DIRTY STORYTELLING
Market with Mud

Nick Winkler

THE WINKLER GROUP
STRATEGIC COMMUNICATIONS

www.thewinklergroup.net

Also by Nick Winkler

Break Out of PR Prison: Make & Measure Your Own
News in an Era of Crisis

Resurrecting TV News: A Digital Plan for the Broadcast
Afterlife

DIRTY STORYTELLING

Market with Mud

Visit **the *Dirty Storytelling*** web site for additional ideas, free handbooks, and resources.

www.dirtystorytelling.com

ISBN-10: 0985789123
ISBN-13: 978-0-9857891-2-1

To Mom & Dad…
For talking dirty to your little boy.
Thank you.
-NRW

CONTENTS

Dirty Storytelling

Nick Winkler

"When you believe, you do."

-Leroy "Satchel" Paige

Nick Winkler

INTRODUCTION

The world never knows quite what to do with relentless.

It's why eventually relentless gets what it desires when a worn down world finally steps aside and yields. People are relentless in their pursuit of truth. Eventually, we'll find what we seek with or without the world's help. If the world, you included, refuses to deliver the truth we demand, we'll simply create truth ourselves. We'll formulate story true to us with or without your input.

Those who refuse to provide truth cede any influence they'd otherwise have over what becomes true to those they wish to delight. But what's true to you may not be true to those you wish to influence. It means telling a story, even one true to you, may not provide your prospects with the truth necessary to inspire them to become customers.

This is the marketer's dilemma.

Even worse, we expect others to believe stories not even we believe. Executives are routinely reminded not to believe their own hype, news release, or marketing. Those who do, the old adage goes, flirt with future failure.

The story often told is unbelievably perfect.

We've been conditioned to sanitize our stories and scrub them of the imperfection we fear. We exaggerate our accomplishments, inflate our qualifications, and fabricate our brands. Doing so gains us acceptance to a university, lands us a job afterward, and determines whether we are promoted later.

We are rewarded for hiding imperfection and simultaneously emphasizing perfection. The mindset bleeds over into our work. We market in a manner consistent with that which resulted in personal success.

But it's no longer working.

The embellished stories we tell are too perfect to be believed. People have learned to ignore story the instant they detect story has been sanitized. Perfectly pristine stories are inconsistent with reality.

The world isn't perfect.

It's why people are skeptical of perfect stories and those who tell them.

Perfectly clean stories create distance between a marketer and prospect. They cause a prospect to wonder what the marketer is hiding. Clean stories erase the benefit of the doubt a prospect wants permission to give the marketer.

People are realistic in terms of fallibility.

Prospects already suspect the marketer is imperfect as we all are. It's only when that imperfection is covered up or whitewashed that a prospect becomes suspicious. The cover up is worse than the crime.

The world is too complex and people are too busy to evaluate the clean stories they are told. So clean stories are ignored and truth is sought elsewhere. It means telling an unbelievable story is like not telling one at all.

Telling no story at all would at least save you the time and money wasted telling clean stories. It would also prevent the ill will a prospect inevitably feels toward those who delay or temporarily prevent her pursuit of truth.

The truth we seek is dirty.

It is found in an individual or organization's reaction to the imperfect. The truth people desire is illuminated by the reaction to conflict, adversity, and dilemma. How an individual or organization navigates challenges, mistakes, and obstacles helps us decide if they're right for us.

We want to see what you do when you don't know what to do. We want you to reveal how you respond to the fear, uncertainty, and doubt we all experience at some point. And we want you to disclose these revelations in ways that benefit us. Disclosing imperfection for our benefit will earn you our attention, belief, and business.

These are dirty stories.

- *Dirty stories* are generous revelations of imperfection that promise to benefit others, arouse the emotional co-creation of story, and inspire and empower others to spread story.
- *Clean stories* are unbelievably perfect, conflict-free broadcasts, and are created for the risk-free benefit of the storyteller.

Dirty stories are in a category of their own.

They are to be courageously embedded in your marketing, public relations, and internal communications.

Dirty stories allow you to use imperfection to help others attain pleasure or avoid pain. Not every story you tell must be dirty. But the belief dirty stories inspire will cause the rest of your communications to become more credible.

Dirty stories are not racy, offensive, or profane. They are authentic and sincere attempts to provide truth to those relentlessly seeking it. However, they require much of those telling them.

Dirty storytellers will experience the discomfort, unease, and fear that naturally come from being vulnerable publicly. Telling dirty stories requires that you ignore conventional marketing wisdom. The personal risk a dirty storyteller takes is rewarded with belief.

Your marketing health hinges upon inspiring belief that spreads. But the perfectly clean stories you believe are safe to tell are actually killing you.

The ideas in this book may save your marketing life.

Dirty Storytelling

THE STORYTELLER'S DILEMMA: DIRTY VS. CLEAN

The clean stories you tell have been sanitized and scrubbed of everything that make them believable and worthy of spreading.

SUICIDE BY STORY

The stories you're telling are killing you.

They're perilously perfect and work to create an invisible crisis that grows silently. A crisis that is likely to reveal itself only after it's too late to mitigate.

Even worse, the innovative and creative ways you tell your stories are actually jeopardizing your success, putting your financial health at risk, and sabotaging your future.

Your storytelling protects your reputation, bolsters your brand, and galvanizes your image. The beautiful narratives you create spotlight people, processes, and prowess of which anyone should envy. But the better you become at telling the stories you tell, the greater the danger you create.

You're executing flawlessly.

It should scare the hell out of you.

But it doesn't.

You've become a master at designing, creating, and distributing perfectly pristine stories to customers, the media, and even your own employees. Your mental agility has enabled you to smartly pivot with changes in technology. Your eagerness to adapt has allowed you to dramatically scale your storytelling strategy.

You're performing exactly as you've been told you should.

It's why you're in trouble.

You've earned pay, praise, and promotion for the efficiency gains you've achieved, platforms you've dominated, and automation you've conquered. The polished narratives you weave earn plaudits from traditional marketers, public relations professionals, and internal communications gurus.

You are an elite teller of the stories you tell.

Eventually, your greatness will kill you.

The perfectly clean stories you routinely include in your marketing, public relations, and internal communications have been stripped of that which makes them intriguing, believable, and spreadable. In fact, you habitually remove the very elements which would cause your story to connect, persuade, and influence those who really count—prospects and customers.

You're a victim of your own success.

Your storytelling is likely thriving internally. Your boss, her boss, and your marketing peers are infatuated with the stories you tell, your message control, and the strategic positioning they believe it all creates.

These aren't the people who matter though.

Outside your bubble of safety and praise are those who do matter—your prospects and customers. To them the majority of the stories you tell are irrelevant, invisible, or ignorable. More importantly, the stories you tell to them simply aren't believable.

Why?

They're perfect.

Marketers have become so good at what they do they are no longer believed by many of the people they wish to influence. Professional storytellers are so effective at polishing, positioning, and prefacing that their expertise actually works to undermine their credibility.

More concerning is most aren't even aware there's a problem.

Your perceived prowess as a storyteller has been derived from the wrong sources. That which serves to complement, elevate, or reinforce the majority of your current storytelling is suicidal. It's as if you're playing Russian roulette with the stories you tell. No matter how fortunate you are now, one day the unbelievable stories you tell will kill you or the dream you're trying to turn into a reality.

The more effective you become at telling the perfect stories you tell, the sooner you'll meet your fate. The stories you tell may impress the people they serve to flatter, but those aren't the people who count. You may be recognized by your co-workers, colleagues, and cohorts, but it's little more than self-idolatry.

The perfection you've achieved in story is killing you. It is simply unbelievable.

You're just too clean for your own good.

CLEAN KILLS

We're literally cleaning ourselves to death.

Thousands of people will die this year, just as they do every year, in pursuit of the illusion of cleanliness. Our fatal obsession with cleanliness often prompts us to scrub, scour, and sanitize our bodies of the very things that promote health.

Ridding our world entirely of dirt comforts us cognitively but actually prevents us from developing immunities that would otherwise protect and strengthen our health. Even worse, we over-sanitize our lives in ways that strengthen that which aims to make us sick. In fact, we abuse that which does cleanse us of disease in ways that ultimately harm and make us sicker.

For instance, our overuse of antibiotics has created superbugs which are antibiotic-resistant. Several of these bugs have mutated or developed genes that enable them to resist multiple antibiotics at once. Diseases that were once easily treated can now be deadly.

Too much clean can kill.

The Centers for Disease Control estimates that each year 2 million people in the U.S. become infected with bacteria that are resistant to antibiotics. Of those infected, 23,000 will die. The CDC says many others die of other ailments complicated by antibiotic-resistant infection.

Using too much of a good thing inevitably causes it to become less potent, desirable, or effective.

The same is true of our marketing.

We scrub our stories of everything that makes them potent. We cleanse, sanitize, and scour them until they're perfect.

But perfect isn't believable.

When we scrub our stories perfect we also make them ignorable, irrelevant, and invisible to the very people for which they are created. Cleansing our stories of imperfection, or the dirt our audience already suspects is there, ensures our stories will not spread.

In marketing, this is the equivalent of dying.

When we tell the world we are nothing but perfect we cause prospects and customers to become skeptical. We plant seeds of doubt in regard to our intentions. They know we're not perfect.

So what are we communicating when we tell them we are?

Over-sanitizing our marketing causes the stories we tell to become belief-resistant. If no one believes your story your business will die, in part, because perfectly clean stories provide no one a reason to believe or talk about you.

Dirty imperfection isn't the enemy.

In fact, it's your dirt that may actually save you.

THE DIRT ON STORY

Not even liars, or people willing to lie to themselves, believe the perfectly clean stories you tell.

Neither do many of you.

In fact, business professionals have conditioned themselves not to believe their own marketing. They routinely joke that believing their own news release is a sign they're in deep trouble. Once you start believing your own hype, the old adage goes, your days as a success are numbered.

But if you don't believe your own marketing why should anyone else?

Once story is sanitized to the point that not even the teller of the story believes it, there's little hope anyone else will buy in.

Why should they?

Belief is in the eye of the believer.

It's difficult enough to identify, find, and convince those we wish to influence that what we truly believe in may also be of value to them. It's easier than ever to ignore believable stories. It's why telling unbelievably clean stories is marketing suicide.

People are willing to believe nearly anything.

Except perfection.

Many of the stories we tell ourselves aren't true.

But truth lies in the stories we tell.

Story dictates trillion dollar swings in the stock market. It heals the sick without medicine. And it predetermines for whom we'll vote despite claims of independence. We believe what we want to believe, actively seek out evidence to support our story, and often tune out anything that contradicts it.

We fool ourselves into believing we are rational.

Into thinking we're right or wrong.

That we can or can't.

When we truly believe the stories we tell ourselves they often come true.

"The medicine is working, I knew I'd get better," we say with a straight face even though the doctor gave us nothing more than a sugar pill.

Dirty Storytelling

"I'll never kick this habit," we tell ourselves despite the tens of thousands before us who have done exactly what we're guaranteeing we cannot.

Whatever it is we believe is likely to be.

Call it the placebo effect, self-fulfilling prophecy, or stubborn persistence.

Whatever you believe it is, it is.

Story is why promises are kept, how revolutions start, and why underdogs win. Belief in the stories we tell provides shortcuts that enable us to make accurate snap decisions, avoid pain, and experience pleasure. It's also responsible for decisions that are never made, an abundance of pain, and a lack of pleasure.

Often, the stories we tell ourselves determine in advance whether we do or don't.

Whether we can or cannot.

Whether we succeed or fail.

It may seem irrational, improbable, or straight crazy but the future that will be is often the one we envision today. It means the story we believe, regardless of whether it's objectively true, is the one that often comes to fruition.

The stories we believe right now are powerful predictors of the future. Understanding what a prospect believes or what she is willing to believe, are insights storytellers must gain prior to telling their story. Only then can a storyteller ask if he is giving those he wishes to influence a story in which they can believe. If so, influencing the story your audience tells itself about your product, service, or offering will dictate whether your business has a future.

If story possesses this much predictive power it's worth examining the stories we routinely tell to those we wish to influence.

Is the story we're telling believable?

It doesn't have to be for everyone.

Just those at whom it is aimed.

Remember, belief is in the eye of the believer.

But when we cleanse our stories of everything that might cause them to be believed we immediately put ourselves at a tremendous disadvantage. If we tell belief-resistant stories not even those predisposed to believe them will.

Even before we can attempt to tell a believable story we must first determine whether the people to whom we want to tell stories want to believe our story. Is your story one they'll cling to in the face of contradictory information? One that confirms and adds to the one they're already telling? One they want to root for, take partial ownership in, and inspires them to tell others about?

Or is the story you're telling perfectly clean?

CLEAN STORIES

Clean stories aren't believable to those at whom they are aimed.

They're belief-resistant and ultimately deadly to your business.

Dirty Storytelling

The tellers of clean stories routinely abide by convention and refrain from believing the perfect stories they tell. Not even they believe their own hype. The problem is the tellers of clean stories are sure they can convince others to believe their unbelievably clean stories.

In essence, marketers of clean stories are saying, "I certainly don't believe this but you should."

Belief must be earned through vulnerability and value.

Not even the richest marketer can force belief. Especially belief in perfectly clean stories. But reality doesn't prevent the fiction in which marketers believe, so they often try to force belief by budgeting for it rather than earning it.

What tellers of clean stories routinely fail to see is that clean stories aren't really stories at all. They are sanitized broadcasts created by and for the narcissists who tell them.

Clean stories are void of conflict, obstacle, and challenge.

They are perfect.

And thus not believable to the rest of the world which knows life isn't perfect. Clean stories are created out of fear. The fear that we'll be exposed as something other than the façades we've created to fool the world.

We all wear masks to cover our imperfections. The masks are in place to protect us from cruelty, criticism, and controversy. More importantly, we wear masks to protect us from ourselves. Our masks are in place to shield us from the imperfection we know is underneath.

Nick Winkler

We spend billions of dollars a year telling stories in the form of advertisements that cover our warts, blemishes, and scars. In reality, our imperfections are the very things that would allow us to stand out and get closer to those we wish to influence. But marketers have been trained to hide these marks of imperfection out of fear that they might become the story should they be revealed.

This fear has blinded marketers to reality.

Story is not imperfection for the marketer brave enough to reveal it on their own and for the benefit of others. Story is actually our reaction to receiving marks of imperfection. It's our reaction to imperfection that actually tells the story of who we are and why others should believe in us.

Our reaction to the imperfect is story.

How we react to conflict is a window through which others may peek to discover our true character. We provide the curious even deeper insight when we disclose imperfection for their benefit. Our stories become extremely valuable when our disclosures help others avoid pain or enjoy pleasure.

The majority refuses to make such disclosures out of fear. Marketers mistake a public acknowledgment of imperfection as story rather than their reaction to it. Instead of leveraging vulnerability to create value in our stories we retreat to the familiar and safe—perfectly clean stories.

It's better to keep our masks on, we're told. It's safer to avoid being vulnerable. And it's definitely more efficient and less risky.

But it's also a guarantee we won't be believed.

WHY CLEAN STORIES NO LONGER WORK

It's human nature to hide fault and highlight strength. It's how we survive.

Evolutionary history aside, marketers have also been conditioned to hide fault. Before technology shattered the traditional media's captive audience into millions of niches, slivers, and pockets, clean stories worked.

Sanitize your story. Scrub it of everything imperfect or dirty. And force feed it to an audience that is unable to change, challenge, or choose otherwise.

Clean stories were swallowed because the audience of yesterday lacked choice, ability, and authority. The audience was manipulated to feel inadequate. Afterward, the storytelling hero would swoop in with the magic cure.

In a bygone era, storytellers were heroes because they said they were heroes.

Technology has tilted the balance of power though.

Now you're only a hero if someone else says you are and others believe it.

Storytellers can no longer force people to pay attention or buy what they're selling. The once powerless audience that has been shattered to pieces, Humpty Dumpty, is not likely to be put back together again.

But modern storytellers haven't changed their tact much.

Sure, they market with humor now rather than inadequacy, but they're still telling clean stories.

Perfect stories.

The kind that don't command attention, earn trust, or spread.

Clean stories are fraudulent.

They are lies of omission.

Remember, people are happy to believe in lies they want to believe. The type that support their worldview or allow them to believe they are rational and consistent.

But they will not believe the lies the majority of marketers tell.

Why?

A trust deficit exists.

Business leaders are distrusted more than any other group besides politicians. The clean stories they tell are partially responsible for the mistrust. Repetitively perfect messaging is simply not consistent with our experiences in life.

No one believes perfect stories.

It's why perfect stories, those that have been cleansed of everything that might make them authentic, are irrelevant, invisible, and ignored.

Even by people willing to believe lies.

CLEAN STORYTELLERS ARE AFRAID

They're afraid of being vulnerable.

They're concerned exposing their imperfections publicly will stamp them as failures, underperformers, or as unreliable. The tellers of clean stories are shortsighted in their perceptions. They misunderstand imperfection and its role in story.

The trust deficit mentioned earlier works both ways.

Clean storytellers do not trust those to whom they are telling stories. Instead of trusting they'll be forgiven should they err while attempting to delight, clean storytellers play it safe and do not risk trying to delight. Rather than use their vulnerabilities to create value for others, they shy away from the authenticity required to erase the trust deficit.

I'm attacking a narrow but extremely important aspect of marketing here. I'm asking you to examine the fear you have that causes you to whitewash your marketing materials. The pitches, brochures, and news releases that ignore elephants like:

- Obstacles
- Mistakes
- Failure

Clean stories are born, in part, of assumptions that have not been challenged. Assumptions that create distance between you and those you wish to influence.

Assumptions that make your story difficult to believe and easy to ignore:

- People buy from the strong not the vulnerable
- People buy from the sure not the unsure
- People buy from the correct not the mistaken

These assumptions are true if you believe them.

But are they true all the time?

More importantly, do those you wish to influence believe these assumptions are universal, absolute, and omnipresent?

No doubt you are strong, sure, and correct.

But at times aren't you also vulnerable, unsure, and mistaken?

Sure you are.

And it's your response to these challenges that provide you the ingredients needed to tell a story that's believable.

But highlighting our response means acknowledging the imperfect.

This is what we fear.

And it's why the majority mindlessly default to clean storytelling.

Clean stories are cliché & void of conflict. They are whitewashed versions of reality that are inconsistent with our understanding of an imperfect world.

If they were movies, they'd be Hollywood stinkers.

Clean stories are the kind with which cowards market. While they guarantee the storyteller won't scrape her elbow, they also ensure she won't leave the mark she desires.

If you ignore the challenges, obstacles, and conflict you've overcome, expect others to ignore you.

CLEAN IS CLICHÉ

It won't get you in trouble but it won't get you noticed.

It ignores the negative and the courage it takes to overcome it.

It bleeds insincerity but will never infect.

It is safe but not trusted.

THE CLEAN STORYTELLER'S SIN

- Boring
- Fake
- Expected
- Arrogant
- Insincere
- Selfish

YOUR IPOD IS DIRTY

But not the kind of dirt you want to wash away.

Dirt is truth.

Your songs, at least the ones that touch you, are dirty in some way.

Not unclean.

Or negative.

But dirty in the sense that they reveal themselves to you in ways that cause you to internalize the story you

28

are hearing. They prompt you to own a piece of the story. You believe in them because they are yours.

Your favorite songs reveal truths in unexpected ways. They surprise you with honesty and art.

Think about your favorites.

Are they songs about perfection?

Or trouble-free tales of bliss, blessedness, and beatitude?

Or might your favorites include loss, struggle, and heartache? The songs we love often showcase a world knocked out of balance and a quest to restore balance. During the quest, our favorite songs expose us to conflict and the resolution of that conflict.

They may not end the way we want.

They might end with surprise.

But we are satisfied with the truth they reveal.

Our favorites are time stamps and allow us to go back and visit places or people. We remember the lyrics years later. And we feel a little of what we felt when we first heard them.

How can our favorite songs be so powerful?

In part, because they're not spotless.

The imperfect story is perfectly believable.

THE STORYTELLER'S STAGE

Vulnerability is the stage on which we should tell some of our stories.

I realize livelihoods turn on strength.

I'm not asking you to be weak.

Dirty Storytelling

I'm urging you to show your strength by being vulnerable.

I know, you're not allowed to be vulnerable at work. The vulnerable don't get promotions, pay raises, or plaudits. These are reasons why vulnerability is rarely exhibited publicly in the stories we tell. If it's not okay to be vulnerable internally, why would it be acceptable anywhere else?

Understand I'm not advocating being vulnerable without reason. I'm urging you to be purposefully vulnerable. Use vulnerability in story to create value for the benefit of others. Teach them how to avoid pain or grasp pleasure.

Marketers who stop shying away from the stage of vulnerability will be rewarded with trust, belief, and attention.

Understand vulnerable simply means being susceptible to harm.

It doesn't mean weak.

Vulnerability is a stage that provides an opportunity to be brave. Brave in the way we handle adversity, conflict, and the threat of harm.

It's on this stage that we are afforded an opportunity to prove our strength, expertise, and prowess.

Vulnerability is the storyteller's stage.

It is an asset.

Vulnerability is an asset when used purposefully, strategically, and subtly. It certainly does not require telling your boss a deep dark secret with which you're wrestling. It's not a tearful television confession, a monetary donation to those you've offended, or a dramatic marketing mea culpa, though it can be.

It's about providing the world a reason to believe you. It is about leveraging your vulnerability for the benefit of others. It's about using imperfection to create value for others.

Telling stories from the stage of vulnerability allows an audience to size you up. It enables a listener to measure and compare the intangible. It allows us to see what you're made of under pressure.

The story isn't that you are vulnerable.

It's how you react to being vulnerable.

The strong, secure, and confident generate a return on their vulnerability when they provide those they wish to influence an opportunity to measure their grit.

It's not the whole story.

And not one you must tell every time.

But purposefully weaving vulnerability into your stories will catch the world off guard. Convincing the world to momentarily drop its guard and pay attention is a prerequisite for believing and spreading your idea.

No one who matters lets their guard down for clean stories though.

Fear keeps clean storytellers from hopping on the stage of vulnerability.

It's comfortable and safe to avoid the stage.

Stage fright is costly though.

Vulnerability is an asset.

It's this simple.

And equally frightening.

THE DIRT ON LIES

I used to think my job as an investigative television news reporter was to figure out who was lying to me before deadline.

Then I realized everyone was lying to me.

Not in the sense that they were deliberately misleading me, though some did.

But I came to realize the stories people tell themselves aren't necessarily true even though they are true to the people telling them.

These were the stories they were telling me during interviews.

And these were the stories I condensed and told on live television.

It meant I was lying as well.

The lies we tell ourselves help us make sense of a complex world. In the absence of certainty we simply fill in the blanks and tell ourselves a story that makes sense to us. The majority of this is done subconsciously.

We use story as a shortcut to create meaning.

It's how we navigate a world that offers us more data than we can process.

The decisions we make are often based on emotion. Afterward, we seek out information to justify our decisions.

More importantly, we seek out evidence that shows our decision was the right one.

Once we create stories we believe it's hard to part with them.

It's difficult to admit they might not be correct.

We're told being consistent is virtuous.

Changing our minds, even in the face of overwhelming contradictory evidence, makes us flip-floppers.

And flip-floppers don't get re-elected.

So we tell ourselves lies that support the stories we've been telling. We actively seek out information that confirms the story we tell ourselves. And we simultaneously ignore or dismiss information that would contradict our story.

When is the last time you changed someone's mind?

I mean on a grand stage.

Have you ever changed someone's mind about abortion? Convinced the opposition to vote for your candidate? Or gotten the driver of a Ford pickup to switch to a Chevrolet?

Maybe, but reversals like these are infrequent.

It means your story, even one that is true to you, is irrelevant to many.

They'll often ignore it if it doesn't reinforce or add to theirs. This means even those who disclose imperfection for the benefit of others may not be believed by those they wish to influence. Even those who tell believable stories that create value will be ignored or not believed by people who deem these stories as inconsistent with those they're already telling themselves.

Even marketers with a great story will fail if they tell it to the wrong people.

Dirty Storytelling

This is why clean storytellers fail universally. The unbelievably perfect stories they tell don't resonate with anyone. A teller of clean stories creates a disadvantage that cannot be overcome.

Why?

Perfectly clean stories are meaningless or irrelevant to everyone but the narcissists who tell them.

They take into account no one's story but their own.

Clean stories are guaranteed to be ignored by nearly everyone because the teller ignores the stories her audience is already telling itself.

Only those willing to invest in understanding the story those they wish to influence are already telling have a chance of connecting with a story that leverages vulnerability to create value.

Understanding their story is a prerequisite to spreading yours.

First, identify the people who are willing to listen and believe.

These are the ones to whom we talk dirty.

Nick Winkler

THE DIRTY STORYTELLING MODEL

Dirty stories are generous revelations of imperfection and disclosed for the benefit of others and those they influence.

THE DIRTY STORYTELLING MODEL

Dirty stories command attention and stand out because they are vibrantly authentic and are told for the benefit of someone other than the teller.

The Dirty Storytelling Model consists of four main components that overlap or combine in ways that help marketers achieve their storytelling objectives:

1. Worldview identification
2. Personal revelation
3. Story Co-creation
4. Triggers that spread story

The Dirty Storytelling Model

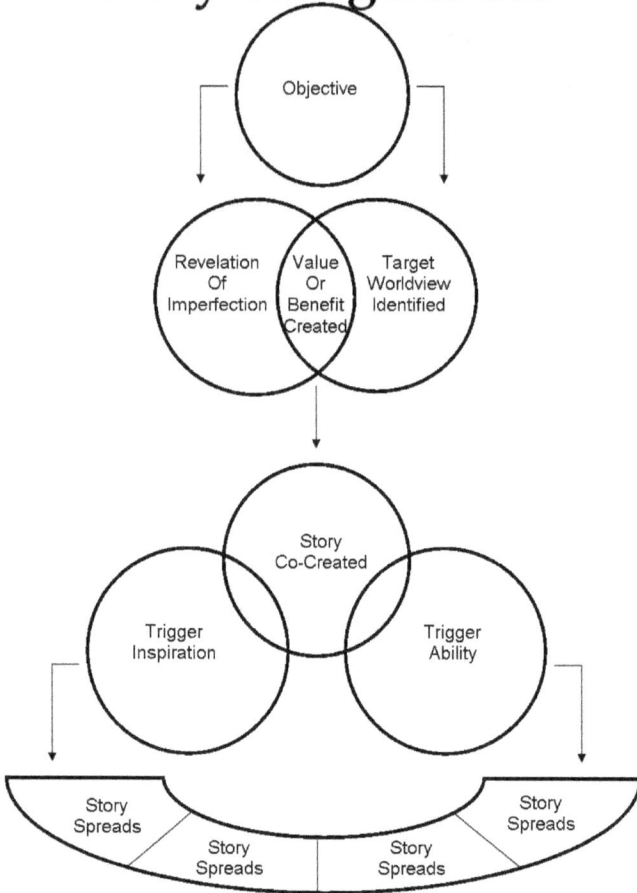

Objective

Revelation Of Imperfection

Value Or Benefit Created

Target Worldview Identified

Story Co-Created

Trigger Inspiration

Trigger Ability

Story Spreads

Story Spreads

Story Spreads

Story Spreads

Each component, along with various techniques you'll use to execute a plan, will be outlined in greater detail in the sections to come. Additionally, each section will also be followed by a worksheet you can use to develop dirty stories of your own.

  For now though, a brief overview of the model is provided.

DIRTY STORIES DEFINED

Dirty stories are generous revelations of imperfection that promise to benefit others, arouse the emotional co-creation of story, and inspire and empower others to spread story.

- Dirty stories are promises
- Promises reveal truth
- Truth exposes true character
- True character is revealed by conflict
- Response to conflict arouses emotion
- Emotion enables the co-creation of story
- Co-created stories are believable and spread

The following are brief descriptions of the model's four main components.

I. YOUR DIRTY CUSTOMERS (WORLDVIEW)

Your prospects and customers tell themselves stories about you regardless of whether you're involved in the creation of those stories. Before you can begin creating compelling stories that resonate and spread among those you wish to influence, you must first identify the stories they're already telling themselves or their worldviews. You may not like these stories. They may not be flattering. But understanding the truths held by those you wish to influence is a prerequisite to changing how they feel and ultimately their behavior. Identifying these stories is not always easy. Much of our decision making occurs beneath the surface of awareness. It's why focus groups will not likely yield the data you need. People often do not consciously understand why they behave as they do. Or at the very least they are often unable to accurately convey these reasons verbally. Identifying inaccurate worldviews is the same as ignoring them altogether. Observing, probing, and engaging in alternative worldview identification techniques will serve as a foundation for dirty storytelling.

II. SLING MUD (REVELATION)

Strategically revealing the existence of an imperfection immediately differentiates your story. Revelation is the mud you sling. Admissions of imperfection are rare. It's why they stand out and command attention. They violate expectations and surprise. Revealing a conflict, controversy, or challenge reduces the distance between you and those you wish to influence. Doing so signals you trust your audience in a way others do not. When you sling mud you are trusting your audience with a secret others are not willing to tell. People entrusted with secrets develop an affinity for the secret provider. Trust is more likely to be reciprocated when a storyteller is perceived as being trusting, honest, and proactively forthcoming. Acknowledging the imperfection your audience already suspects exists earns you a degree of credibility clean storytellers are not afforded. The revelation is not the story. The story is how you respond to the imperfection and how others may benefit. Revelations allow the teller to dramatize the narrative. Without drama others have little reason to listen or care. It's why clean stories are ignored or not believed. Admissions allow those you wish to influence to discover on their own your true character.

III. SLING MUD TOGETHER (CO-CREATION)

If we do not tell a compelling story we will be ignored. If we do not tell an authentic story we will not be believed. If those we wish to influence do not believe the story we tell they will certainly not be inspired to spread our story. Instead, they'll create their own stories independent of ours. The stories they create may or may not be favorable to us. Therefore, creating an environment in which we can co-create story with our audience is important. Co-creation is the equivalent of slinging mud alongside your audience. Co-creating story means those we wish to influence have an ownership stake in our story. Your audience will be helping to create the proof by which it is convinced when it co-creates story with you. Your response to conflict under increasing pressure will dramatize your narrative. Drama creates intrigue and stimulates your target's imagination in a manner that inspires co-creation. Audiences will care much more deeply about a narrative they help create.

IV. TRIGGER A MUDSLIDE (SPREAD)

An audience that is emotionally invested in your story is more likely to tell others. Word of mouth marketing is the mudslide you wish to trigger. Your job as a co-creator is to inspire and empower your audience to spread the story. This is done by embedding easy to squeeze triggers throughout story. Your story must come equipped with triggers that enable it to spread. Triggers motivate and provide a functional way to spread your story. Embedded triggers may be subtle or conspicuous depending on the context. Those you wish to influence should be able to easily pull these triggers and spread story.

WHAT ARE DIRTY STORIES?

Dirty stories aren't meant to replace all of your stories.
  Dirty storytelling is a category in and of itself. Dirty stories are marketing bolt-ons. They are tools to be used to inspire belief.
  Dirty stories are to be strategically embedded throughout your organization's communications. They

are subtle and not so subtle reminders as to why your audience should believe in you.

Dirty stories cannot be faked, manufactured, or spun. Life isn't always clean.

Dirty stories respect this fact of life and the people who tell them respect their audiences in a manner that differentiates them. Dirty storytellers channel misfortune, misdeed, and missed opportunity into something that may benefit others. They begin relationships with those they wish to influence with authenticity.

Dirty storytellers elevate their audiences. The trust they place in their audience by being vulnerable for its benefit is often reciprocated and earns admiration clean storytellers do not.

Dirty stories aren't necessarily stories in the traditional sense.

Not all of them contain heroes who are knocked off balance and set out on dramatic quests chock-full of conflict to restore balance in ways that result in dramatic and irreversible change.

Dirty stories are both bombastic and subtle. They may take the form of:

- Product packaging
- Positioning
- Brand tag choice
- Design elements
- Customer service choices
- How you answer the phone

- Your warranty
- Return policies
- Social engagement
- Waiting room music
- How & when you communicate
- Sales strategy
- Presentations
- Earned media
- Advertising
- Where you market

You can become a dirty storyteller in a variety of ways.

Critics will argue airing dirty laundry is dangerous and risky.

It is but you're only rewarded when you take risks.

Understand dirty storytellers take calculated risks.

A veterinarian doesn't have to tell the world about the pet that died during surgery. A surgeon doesn't need to volunteer how he amputated the wrong finger. And a restaurant doesn't need to announce it failed its last health department inspection.

There is a line between dirty and suicidal.

Realize though the closer your marketing takes its audience to that line the greater the odds your audience will tell others about you.

So what do dirty stories look like in the real world?

Here's how some of the best market with mud:

- The first line of Britten Follett's child abuse prevention speech in which she shows a picture

44

of a two and a half year-old victim of child abuse and inspires her audiences to make the topic a political issue, "I killed this little girl- we all did!"

- The "This Can't be a Buick" television commercial the car company uses to ridicule and change its boring reputation by spotlighting the humorous reaction grandmothers have to new Buick offerings.

- The documentary in which Domino's Pizza admits its product tastes, "…like cardboard…and ketchup…" and tests its reinvented pizza on critics.

- The title of Scott Adams' book, *How to Fail at Almost Everything and Still Win Big.*

- Gini Dietrich's public relations blog and book, *Spin Sucks.*

- The milk cartons in which Seth Godin packaged *Purple Cow.*

- The vans Spirit Airlines packs with female dancers to promote flights to Vegas.

- The first line of Roger Creager's song "Crazy Again," "My boss is a son of a bitch"…and the subsequent admissions that inspire listeners to stand up for what is right rather than popular.

- Child behavioral therapist Janet Lehman's marketing materials which include her radio admission, "I'll never forget the day my child told me they hated me!"

Dirty Storytelling

Each of these dirty storytellers takes a calculated risk. And each has been rewarded in some way.

The story is not the revelation but the teller's reaction to it. Each dirty story listed is a success because each leaves people with little choice but to tell others.

It matters little whether these dirty stories impressed you. They aren't aimed at everyone. They're meant only for people who might be willing to listen to and believe the story being told.

The selected sliver and its reaction is what matters.

Criticism and complaints from those outside the sliver do no damage. In fact, they often rally the dirty storyteller's base and draw more attention to the story.

Remember, I mentioned dirty stories can take a variety of forms. The examples I provided earlier are traditional types of stories: commercials, speeches, and books.

But dirty stories don't have to be traditional. In fact, they don't even require words. The dirty story that follows is unorthodox. But notice the necessary elements are present despite the story being void of words.

THE DIRTY STORY THAT CLEANED A BATHROOM

Kim Bartmann's business card says she's an instigator. She is but she's also a fixer who uses dirty stories to solve problems.

Bartmann owns and runs a handful of restaurants in Minneapolis and is known for her business acumen, managerial prowess, and ability to balance it all. But Bartmann also stands out as a leader because of the unorthodox way she uses dirty storytelling to solve a genuinely dirty problem- bathroom graffiti.

Night after night Bartmann found her bathroom walls covered with the drunken art of last night. It costs her time and money to scrub, cover, and wash what always turns into the next day's ugly mess.

Some restaurant owners see bathroom graffiti as a cost of doing business and ignore the problem until it's time to cover it up. Others appeal to customers' consciences but often lose late night battles like these.

Bartmann no longer does either.

In a stroke of dirty creativity Bartmann flipped the problem and constructed a dirty story without a single word.

She now invites graffiti artists to mark up her bathrooms.

Why?

Dirty Storytelling

She changed the rules and hung chalk boards on her bathroom walls and now urges customers dying to express themselves artistically to write, scribble, and draw. She even supplies chalk to those who see her bathroom walls as their personal easels.

The dirty story being told here, without a word, is, "Be my guest graffiti artist! I'll help you leave your mark on the world. It just won't be a permanent one my staff has to spend time and money wiping away."

The bathroom chalkboards are often topics of conversation when customers return to their tables. They've also earned Bartmann the respect of graffiti artists who admire her creativity.

Even though the story lacks a single word it contains the elements necessary to make it effective:

- Customer worldview identified
- A silent revelation is made
- Co-creation is stimulated
- Word of mouth triggered

The chalk boards have even become places on which customers leave inspirational quotes, song lyrics, or otherwise amusing pieces of culture. In other words, they've given even those who never intended to be graffiti artists something to talk about.

It's a dirty story that literally cleaned up a bathroom.

Ready to try slinging some mud yourself?

How about injecting some dirt into a good 'ol fashion crisis?

Dirty storytelling is a smart way to disarm angry customers.

For instance, if General Motors wanted to tell a dirty story following revelations in 2014 it did not issue a recall for vehicles with faulty ignitions that resulted in multiple deaths despite knowing the ignitions were faulty, it could do so via its customer service.

It's a tongue-in-cheek example, but what if GM's customer service representatives tasked with handling inquiries answered the phones by telling this dirty story:

"Hi there! If you're calling about the car we sold you with the junk ignition, I'm sorry. We should've told you immediately but didn't want to spend the money. We're making it right though and that starts with this call. If you want to yell at me, now is the time to do so! If not, I'll answer any questions you might have for me."

Or what if General Motors told a more aggressive dirty story on a different stage? What if it leveled with the public but also provided this dirty truth:

"We want to apologize without excuse to the loved ones of those who died. There's no excuse for installing ignitions we knew were faulty at the time. There's also no excuse for drinking and driving. While we regret our mistake, we also regret that some of the drivers who

died in these instances had been drinking alcohol prior to getting behind the wheel."

General Motors would never answer the phone this way or make such an announcement.

But doing so would immediately disarm angry callers and provide the public a more complete picture of the circumstances surrounding the controversy. Telling a dirty story would be risky in both scenarios. However, doing so would also communicate understanding, empathy, and honesty.

Neither scenario, on its own, would be an appropriate way to communicate with victims' families. And GM's lawyers would likely never allow dirty stories like these to be told.

The company will undoubtedly experience severe financial consequences. Dirty stories won't make those consequences any better or worse.

But marketing with a little mud can immediately begin repairing broken trust by honestly acknowledging the elephants in the room.

Dirt isn't a cure-all.

But it's a start toward rebuilding trust and belief.

WHO TELLS DIRTY STORIES?

Only people with courage, conviction, and confidence.

Saviors like Jesus Christ.

Billionaires, paupers, and professional cage fighters tell dirty stories too.

Slinging mud can be uncomfortable, risky, and counterintuitive.

It's why dirty storytellers are rare.

It's also why they stand out, make history, and win.

You need guts to market with mud.

Do you want to become one of us?

If so you'll become part of a rare breed of storyteller. Like the *Dirty Storytelling Hall of Famers* who are featured on page 172.

But before you go…

TAKE THE TEST

Are you a clean storyteller?

Do you routinely sanitize your marketing by scrubbing it of the very elements that would endear your offering to those for whom it is meant?

The majority of marketing today is clean.

Rose colored glasses are the only kind through which most marketers are taught to look. Brand managers, reputation management gurus, and public relations professionals have been trained to add story at the end. Story is an afterthought. Fix the product or service with story in post.

But when the story isn't believable, what are you fixing?

Even more concerning, what are you accomplishing?

Dirty storytelling requires you to remove the rose colored glasses. It demands an honest assessment of your shortcomings. And it insists you remedy your maladies publicly.

Dirty Storytelling

The majority play it safe though.
Do you?
Are you a clean storyteller?
Take this test to find out.

THE CLEAN STORYTELLER TEST

Do you routinely:

- Hide controversy from your audience?
- Minimize the consequences of mistakes?
- Omit potentially damaging information?
- Dump a negative news release late Friday afternoon?
- Refuse to return a reporter's call?
- Ignore a customer service issue by blaming the customer?
- Inquire as to why journalists do not feel your last news release was newsworthy?

If you answered any of these questions in the affirmative you're likely a clean storyteller.
  Congratulations, you're in the majority.
  Clean storytellers are in abundant supply.
  The problem is clean stories are not in demand.
  They do not generate a return.
  They're also costly.
  If you've never been a bit frightened, unsure, or uncomfortable prior to telling a story, you've never told a dirty story.

WHY YOU DON'T TELL DIRTY STORIES (AT LEAST PUBLICLY)

Dirty stories require you to let go.

They demand you cede a bit of the control you believe you have over your story.

They insist you trust your audience with the brand you've spent so much money creating, nourishing, and protecting.

Clean storytellers do not have these uncomfortable problems.

Those who tell clean stories believe they alone control their message. Traditional marketing taught us this. The broadcast age and its captive audience reinforced this belief. But the control clean storytellers enjoyed for so long was only temporary.

Now control is an illusion.

If clean storytellers want to maintain a death grip on their message they certainly can. But that message will belong to them and only them. They'll maintain the illusion of control.

But they won't have a story.

And certainly not one that spreads.

The truth is clean storytellers generally fit one of these three personas:

1. The Bully
2. The Narcissist
3. The Clueless

Clean stories are ideal for those of you who still believe you can force-feed an audience or for those concerned only about search engine optimization.

Perfectly clean stories are also ideal for those who want to read glowing news releases about themselves.

They're also adequate for those who haven't yet updated their skill sets.

If any of these personas describe you then clean stories are a good fit. You'll get just what you asked for, you'll maintain the illusion of control, and you'll feel safe, secure, and good about yourself.

Make sure you have deep pockets though.

Clean storytellers spend a lot of money marketing to people who ignore them.

There's a more efficient way though.

But it requires letting go of your story.

You'll lose control.

You'll be judged.

You'll be critiqued.

But your story just might be believed and spread.

DIRTY STORIES SAVE YOU MONEY

Clean stories are expensive ways to fail.

They reinforce an audience's decision to ignore you, prove you are a narcissist, and provide a reason to choose a competitor.

Outside firms are happy to take your money and mass blast clean but irrelevant stories to prospects, reporters, and lists. However, when you mass blast clean stories to the masses you won't generate a robust return.

The Havas Media Group recently conducted a research project and found those surveyed would not care if 73% of the world's brands ceased to exist.

It means there's a lot of money being wasted playing it safe.

Dirty storytellers reverse the process.

They invest in story at the outset. They design it into their offering and reduce their marketing costs on the back end.

They understand the world has come full circle, that word of mouth is once again king.

People do not buy our products or services.

They buy our stories.

But only if our stories are believable.

Sanitized stories are not believable.

PROJECT: BECOME AN ACTIVIST STORYTELLER

Look inward at your storytelling as an activist investor on Wall Street might. Activists identify company inefficiencies, buy shares in the target company, and agitate for efficient change so their shares will increase in value. Would an activist storyteller perceive the stories you tell as efficient, believable, and valuable? Are the stories you tell generating a return in terms of engagement? Find out by answering these questions:

The Activist Storyteller Checklist

1. Are your stories customer-centric or company-centric?
2. Is the content geared toward what you have accomplished?
3. Or is your content geared toward what the customer will achieve?
4. What would your best friend's reaction be should you tell her your story?
5. Does your call to action benefit the customer or just you?

If the stories you tell aren't believable they're not assets. Demand more from your stories and those who tell them. An activist storyteller would not look kindly on clean stories that exist solely to pad egos, feed narcissism, or create the illusion you're standing out.

Dirty storytellers summon the courage necessary to acknowledge imperfection and use it to benefit others and spread their idea.

Offerings that come equipped with powerful stories spread purposefully and organically. They do not require an expensive back end traditional marketing push.

Your job as a storyteller is to inspire people to spread your story to those they influence.

Inspire & empower them.

Do it by slinging mud.

Dirty Storytelling

YOUR CUSTOMERS ARE DIRTY

Understand the dirty stories your customers are telling themselves if you want to tell one they believe and spread.

THE DIRTY STORY THEY TELL

Is more important than the one you want to tell.

What do the people you wish to influence believe? A better question is what do they want to believe? Even better, what do they believe about you?

Remember, people often make decisions based on emotion and then work to justify their decisions afterward. Right or wrong, people seek out evidence that supports their decision while ignoring evidence that might contradict it.

It means you're not going to connect with someone if you're telling a story they are actively trying to ignore. Especially in a world experiencing a brand explosion that throws off more messages in a day than we can possibly spend time thoughtfully evaluating much less comprehend.

It's why people tell themselves stories.

Stories are the shortcuts we use to navigate a complex world packed with information.

These stories contain our biases, beliefs, and values.

They dictate how we see, react to, and make sense of the world.

For instance:

The Benghazi Attack

On September 11, 2012 gunmen attacked the U.S. diplomatic post in Benghazi, Libya. The attack resulted in the death of U.S. Ambassador Christopher Stevens and three others. Initially, it was reported the attack stemmed from a spontaneous protest against an anti-

Muslim YouTube video. Later, it was reported the assault was actually a coordinated terrorist attack by Islamist militants. The administration's response to the attack and statements made thereafter have been sources of fierce debate and controversy as has the topic of media bias.

What do you believe?

Your biases, beliefs, and values will influence how you perceive the Benghazi attack. Regardless of the facts, large portions of the country will perceive the attack differently due to their political biases.

The stories we tell ourselves are why two people can look at the same event and come to starkly different conclusions.

The point is not to jump into storytelling blind or deaf.

You'll waste a lot of time and money not understanding the worldview of your target audience.

Listen to the story they tell themselves.

See it clearly.

HOW IDENTIFYING WORLDVIEWS KEPT ME FROM BEING PUNCHED IN THE LEFT EYE

The old man's lip quivered and his fist shook as he decided whether to punch me in the face.

I was in the middle of nowhere Oregon on assignment as a television news reporter. A toddler had gotten away from his grandparents. He had wandered

Dirty Storytelling

outside for just a moment but when his grandparents found him he was face down in a swimming pool.

The child drowned.

It was my job to travel to the rural home and ask the grieving grandparents if they'd be willing to provide a picture of their grandson and an on camera account of what happened and why the boy would be missed.

After a long drive we parked our news vehicle on the road as a small crowd had gathered in the grandparents' driveway.

I walked up the drive, introduced myself, and was confronted by the grandfather.

He grabbed me by the collar of my shirt, cocked his right arm back so it was ready to punch, and asked, "Tell me why I shouldn't hit you?"

My story was this:

- I don't deserve to be punched
- I'm just doing my job
- All I did was politely ask you to speak with me

My story was legitimate.

It was true.

But I knew it wouldn't be believed or resonate with the grandfather.

So I didn't tell him my story.

Instead, I took a guess at the old man's worldview. I guessed he was telling himself a story about me similar to this:

- This reporter doesn't really care about me, my family, or the loss we're experiencing
- This reporter is here to exploit us on the worst day of our lives
- Even worse, if I do what he wants it may boost his newscast's ratings which may help him charge advertisers more money. He's making money off our tragedy

His story was true.

Just like mine was to me.

Changing someone's worldview is difficult. It's why I didn't try.

So what did I tell the old man after he asked why he shouldn't hit me?

I gave him permission.

I said, "If it'll make you feel better, please do."

Instead of hitting me, the grandfather dropped his fist, began to cry, and hugged me.

Worldviews are powerful.

Ignore them at your peril.

EVEN BUREAUCRATS GET IT

Ever thought about fighting city hall?

It's something you may feel compelled to do at some point if you're in business.

But if you show up at a city council meeting, attend a legislative hearing, or otherwise interact with government officials understand they'll be sizing you up just as I advocate you size up your audience.

Worldview will come into play.

The politicians and bureaucrats with whom you may deal will try to quickly discern your worldview on a specific matter. The idea is to categorize you and others who feel similarly. Once you are categorized bureaucrats will be able to rely on shortcuts to communicate with you.

What do I mean?

They've created personas that help them easily group people they are likely to encounter at city council meetings and the like. Here are two acronyms used to categorize people based on their worldviews:

- **N.I.M.B.Ys**- *Not In My Backyard*- used to describe people opposed to locating things like landfills near their homes
- **C.A.V.ERs**- *Citizens Against Virtually Everything*- used to describe those perceived as opposing anything government supports

Career bureaucrats even have a special persona for the elected officials and appointees with whom they often lock horns and wait out:

- **WEEBIES**- Short for, "We be here longer than you!" It implies that all bureaucrats must do is be patient with problematic elected officials and appointees who'll likely be replaced in an election cycle or two.

These are broad and overly general worldviews.

But they're examples of first understanding worldview before attempting to communicate with the people holding those worldviews.

HOW NOT TO IDENTIFY WORLDVIEWS

Television news loves focus groups.

Stations routinely sit people down, show them newscast clips, and ask them what they do and don't like.

It seems smart but doesn't generally pan out.

How do I know?

I'm familiar with television news stations that have consistently conducted focus groups for years though their newscast ratings continue to fall. I'm not blaming focus groups entirely. There are a variety of factors for the ratings decline.

The lesson here is that television stations routinely ask people what they want. The newsroom then gathers and presents exactly what the viewer said she wanted to see. But the viewer decides not to watch anyway. Traditional focus groups and surveys are not effective in deeply understanding what people believe, why they believe it, and why they act as they do.

Focus groups and surveys are not optimal if you want to thoroughly identify worldviews.

Why?

Dirty Storytelling

We often make snap decisions based on gut feeling. Many of these decisions are made below the surface of awareness. It means we often don't even know or cannot accurately articulate why we do what we do.

We can justify or explain later as we do in focus groups and surveys.

But the answers provided may not be valuable or reliable. Great caution should be used if you're basing expensive product development or brand strategy decisions solely on focus group or survey data.

The fact people know they are being observed colors their answers as well.

There's also the risk that a single participant dominates the discussion or speaks in a manner that causes other participants to alter their views or keep them to themselves.

Worldviews may be discerned in a number of ways depending on the context and what you're trying to accomplish.

Focus groups and surveys may be helpful at times.

It's possible they might effectively identify a worldview accurately enough in situations that require less probing.

But beware of focus group limitations for more complex storytelling or branding projects.

The veracity and predictive power of the data focus groups produce should be viewed more skeptically than is often the case.

Nick Winkler

THE SECRET TO IDENTIFYING WORLDVIEWS

Is avoiding gorgeous women.

I'm only partially kidding.

I worked with gorgeous women in television newsrooms across the country for 15 years. It's why interview subjects, especially men, routinely volunteered to travel to my television stations to be interviewed.

Often, they simply wanted an opportunity to meet the women of the newsroom.

I always declined their generous offers though and met them at their home locations.

Why?

It wasn't to deprive them of what they desired. My intention was to identify their attitudes, beliefs, and values by observing them in their environments. I would be at a distinct disadvantage if I were to allow interviewees to come to me.

By quickly scanning an interviewee's home or office environment I learned a bit about what they believed. This information allowed me to better choose small talk topics and frame questions in ways that produced better interview sound. Better sound makes for better television news.

- Family pictures
- Books
- Decorations

- Jewelry
- Vehicle type

These items often told me what interview subjects likely would or could not. They often exposed an interviewee's biases, beliefs, and values. They spoke for the interview subject. They provided the background a stranger is often not initially inclined to provide.

It's why observing prospects and customers in their environments is so important in identifying worldviews.

Focus groups don't do this.

Neither do surveys.

Observing those you wish to influence in their environments will often tell you more than they will. In other words, read the cards. They'll tell you what people often won't or can't.

Here's a more sophisticated way of unearthing the hidden treasure of worldviews:

Metaphor Elicitation- Gerald Zaltman of Harvard details this technique in *How Customers Think*. Zaltman says our thoughts are largely based on images rather than words. It's why uncovering the hidden thoughts and feelings we have, those that are created below the surface of awareness, is difficult to do with language-based collection techniques. Instead, Zaltman argues we'll better understand customers if we ask them to create visual stories or collages based on what they believe. The metaphors or pictures they choose to represent their beliefs will often provide meaning people cannot with their words.

If asking prospects to draw or bring you pictures that represent how they feel about a subject isn't what you're after, here are several additional options:

- Observational Research
    1. Covert
    2. Overt
    3. Researcher participation
- Interrogation (one on one interviews)
- Active Listening
- Ethnography
- Anthropology

Empathy is the key to identifying the stories people tell themselves no matter which tactic you choose to use.

Empathy requires you to ignore your story, product, or service and look at the world through the eyes of your customers. See what they see. Experience what they experience. Feel what they feel.

We're all capable of this.

It's why we cringe when our favorite fighter is punched, when our favorite baseball pitcher takes a line drive off the shin, or when our favorite cyclist crashes badly onto the pavement.

David and Tom Kelley are the geniuses who wrote *Creative Confidence* and talk at length about empathy and how it will help you understand that your customer, not your product, is the hero in the story being told. Your product is simply the mentor, secret weapon, or aid that will help your customer be a hero and achieve their dreams.

Empathy allows us to truly understand the personal dramas in which our customers are starring. Our roles in these dramas, if we are smart and lucky enough to earn them, will be only as supporting actors.

Our role is to aid the hero in her quest to achieve her goal.

We aren't the hero.

We are the hero's helper.

It means clean storyteller's have it backward.

LEVERAGING THE WORLDVIEW

You ignore one specific story routinely.

The one the snoring older gentleman on your right is also ignoring.

And the one the millennial wearing noise blocking headphones on your left is ignoring too.

It's the FAA mandated safety announcement flight attendants are required to recite prior to taking off in an airplane. Tens of thousands of people ignore this story each day. I feel bad for the flight attendants as they often appear to be in as much agony giving the spiel as passengers are hearing it.

It doesn't have to be this way though.

This FAA mandated message, when turned into a dirty story based on passenger worldviews, is actually a profit center.

Before I illustrate the story, you should understand the context.

It was 5:30 in the morning.

I was one of more than two-hundred people cramming onto a Spirit Airlines flight on a particularly bitterly cold morning.

Spirit, for the uninformed, is a no frills budget carrier that offers ultra-cheap fares in return for less leg room and no freebies.

My fellow passengers, at least the ones who weren't asleep, were grumbling about having to pay for overhead bin space and only half-jokingly asking if they'd be charged for breathing the cabin air.

Time for the FAA mandated safety announcement.

What happened next though was a thing of creative beauty that resulted in commerce.

Spirit recognized the story passengers were telling themselves about the usually mundane announcement and surprised people:

- Your seatbelt should be tighter than a pair of Brittney Spears' jeans
- Should the cabin lose pressure and your oxygen mask deploys, stop screaming and put it on

Dirty Storytelling

One by one, red-eye passengers began waking up and paying attention:

- Should we experience a water landing and you're traveling with children, choose your favorite and give them your flotation device
- While there's no smoking in the cabin our wings are available. At 500 miles an hour if you can light it, smoke it!

Each of the tired and cranky passengers is now laughing and captive. The flight attendant had us in the palm of her hand. She then strikes the knockout blow by addressing the story passengers had been telling themselves about the airline itself:

- Notice the flight attendant call button above you. The first time you press it is free. The second time will cost you $50. After all, you are flying Spirit!

We applauded as we laughed.
She gets it. She understands us. We're in this together.
But the flight attendant's understanding of worldviews did more than prompt a round of applause and goodwill.
Remember, we do business with people we like and trust.

And this was a flight attendant who could be trusted to acknowledge dirty truths in a humorous way that made all of us like her.

It's why it appeared to me passengers were ordering more food and drink items from the flight attendant than is normal for a red-eye flight on a cold morning. As we got off the plane I asked the flight attendant whether my perception was accurate.

It was.

While the flight attendant did not have statistics, she told me a humorous announcement increases a la carte sales substantially versus flights in which the standard FAA mandated announcement is made.

The humor woke people up.

The dirt she slung created a connection.

And none of it would've been possible without first understanding passenger worldviews.

THE DIRTY BRIDGE

Only after you understand the stories people tell themselves about you can you identify ways to plug into their worldviews.

Your job as a storyteller is to build a bridge between you and the prospect or customer. Building a bridge is how you connect your story with theirs. It's finding a way to make your story relevant and believable in the context of their story.

They are the host.

You and your story are the guests.

You want to be invited back for another stay, right?

Dirty Storytelling

If so, don't set out to change their worldview with your story. How successful do you think the Spirit Airlines flight attendant would have been had she tried to convince passengers they had plenty of leg room?

Persuasion occurs on a continuum.

Tossing a *Hail Mary* in terms of trying to change a worldview is not likely to result in success. A believable story plugged into a customer's worldview, even if it's not a comfortably clean story, is more likely to prompt people to move in the direction you desire.

The passengers on the Spirit plane already disliked the lack of leg room.

They already told themselves they were being nickled and dimed despite ultra-low fares.

But they were persuaded to do what they originally complained about which was to spend additional money on a la carte items.

Why?

Spirit had the courage to acknowledge the negative story customers were telling. The airline didn't ignore it. It did not try to change the negative worldview. It simply addressed the worldview in a unique way that changed the way people felt.

The airline framed its story in terms of its passengers' story.

Remember, before people will change how they behave, you have to change how they feel.

WORLDVIEW IDENTIFICATION WORKSHEET

Understanding the beliefs, biases, and values prospects and customers possess will allow you to tell an authentic story that is consistent with and adds to the ones they're already telling.

1. Why do customers use your offering or offerings like yours?

2. Why do they choose one offering in the category over another?

3. What types of opportunities might there be to observe prospects purchasing and using offerings like yours in their natural environments?

4. What do customers believe about the offerings in your category? What frustrates customers about offerings in your category? What do they put up with and what do they hate?

5. What do prospects or customers believe specifically about your offering? Why do they choose or not choose it versus one from a competitor?

Visit www.dirtystorytelling.com to download free copies of this worksheet and new *Dirty Storytelling* resources.

Dirty Storytelling

START SLINGING MUD

Reveal dirty imperfection to the very people you wish to impress and influence.

REVELATION AS STRATEGY

Revealing an imperfection is often the ticket that gets you into the ballpark of attention.

Without the attention of those you wish to influence you won't earn an opportunity to co-create or spread your idea. Revelations may be overt or implied subtly.

Revealing imperfection is generally something we strive to avoid. We're wired to hide imperfections. School reinforces and teaches the notion on a deeper level. And the workplace confirms what we've come to believe; revealing imperfection is risky.

It is risky.

But no one notices safe.

YOUR MARKETING SHOULD SCARE YOU

When was the last time your marketing scared you?

The brochure you weren't sure would work. The news release you were uneasy about. The first line of a speech you knew would be judged.

Ever created something like this?

Please don't define scared as untested. I'm not advocating you blindly let story rip or disregard potential consequences.

I'm referring to the A/B split test that revealed something polarizing in your story. Or the sliver in your email marketing test that responded in an unexpected way. Or the call to action that resulted in an avalanche of conversions. Or none at all.

Storytellers need not be reckless, cavalier, or negligent. But they should be at least slightly afraid.

You have to risk something to be rewarded. Today, that something is not just cash. Clean stories risk nothing. There is nothing at stake except money. The world requires more than that now.

The world insists you put skin in the game.

THE SOURCE OF YOUR FEAR

Should not be your antagonists.

Understand the stone throwers, angry mobs, and character assassins will likely show up in force when you reveal something imperfect.

They'll leave unfounded comments, negative reviews, and launch anonymous attacks.

None of this should frighten you though.

Your attackers aren't the people for whom you've made a revelation.

These are not the people to whom you are speaking.

They're not for whom you're creating story.

Those who attack you for your revelation are likely in possession of the very same imperfection as you. They're just too frightened to reveal it. They don't see the way you see. It's why they'll talk about you.

Be mindful though.

Criticism should not be what makes you afraid of your marketing.

The uncertainty of whether your story will be believed is what should truly frighten you. The decision recipients of your story make in regard to whether they share it should terrify you.

What if they don't believe?

What if they don't tell others?

These are the outcomes you are right to fear.

They determine whether your story has a future.

Not your antagonists.

THE ECONOMICS OF STORY

You owe clean storytellers a kiss.

They're actually partially responsible for your future success as a dirty storyteller.

The economics of story support this.

Clean storytellers are the majority. Which means they work hard to blend in by telling the types of stories they tell. They also spend a lot of money not to stand out.

Clean stories are in abundant supply. The problem is there's little demand for them other than from those ordering that they be told.

Conversely, dirty stories are in short supply. And with consumer trust levels just off their all-time lows, there's tremendous demand for dirty stories. But that demand is often only visible after you take a leap of faith and tell a dirty story.

Will you fill this demand?

The economics of story are clear. Dirty stories are unique.

This is great news for the brave.

We are wired to notice the atypical. We are drawn to anomalies. Our brains automatically focus on the aberrant.

Dirty stories aren't typical.

It means dirty storytellers have an opportunity to earn an oversized amount of the total attention available.

Will you?

REVERSE THE INADEQUACY

I used to scare people into paying attention to me.

As a television news reporter I routinely identified threats, vaguely told people why they were in danger, and teased them into tuning in later for the secret solution I had. You're likely familiar with disingenuous teases like these:

- The danger lurking in your kitchen that could make you sick
- The mysterious threat hiding in your child's crib
- The medication in your cabinet that'll hurt not heal you

What I was really doing was trying to make viewers feel inadequate. I was telling them their kitchens weren't safe, their child's crib was dangerous, and the medicine their doctor prescribed may harm them.

Then, after I identified the problem I swooped in with the magic cure.

The catch is they had to wait for my solution. They'd have to tune in later. I promised to save them but only if they'd help boost my newscast ratings so my station could bilk advertisers out of a few extra bucks.

But if there was really a danger lurking in the kitchen, a crib threat that could hurt a child, or bad medicine in the cabinet, wouldn't the right thing to do be to tell people immediately instead of withholding the information for the sole benefit of the television station?

If not, the threat was exaggerated or I should've been prosecuted.

I soon realized marketers were guilty of similar tactics.

But similar to the dramatic decline in television news ratings and earnings, marketing is paying a price for its behavior as well. Consumers have been empowered by choice and technology.

Television news and marketers no longer have a monopoly on information.

It is infinitely more difficult to manipulate someone who has access to the same information you do.

If we can't force people to pay attention or buy access to information they lack, how might we go about influencing people in a new world?

Reverse the inadequacy.

Instead of abiding by tradition and making others feel inadequate, reveal why you're inadequate at times.

Instead of being a manipulative bully, be vulnerable. Reveal an inadequacy of your own. Share an imperfection that creates value for those you wish to influence. Show them you are willing to be vulnerable for their benefit. Do so to help them avoid a heartache, obstacle, or mistake you've made.

Nick Winkler

If a connection is to be formed with your audience, someone will have to go first. One of you has to make the first move and risk being vulnerable if the goal is reciprocation.

Don't count on the consumer going first though. She has been mistreated by manipulators for some time. He has been fooled by too many lies. It's easier and safer for them to ignore you.

But you can get their attention by reversing the inadequacy.

You are inadequate at times.

You are imperfect.

So start acting like it.

REVELATIONS ARE WRAPPERS

Revelations are emotional wrappers that cloak your message in a coat of believability, authenticity, and reverence.

Nice coat, huh?

Your bullet points, power presentations, and talking points aren't stories. They are key messages. But they aren't likely to be remembered unless they are anchored to emotion.

Revelations wrap your messages in emotion and make them more enjoyable and easier to consume. Revelations provide you an opportunity to attract attention and deliver your key messages subtly through story.

Besides illustrating your courage without words, dirty stories are empowering.

Dirty Storytelling

Political analysts often talk about self-definition. They advise candidates to define themselves before their opponents do it for them. Many believe the candidate who first defines her opponent creates an advantage with voters. You're in trouble, analysts contend, if the opposition is responsible for defining you in the minds of voters:

- Flip-flopper
- Compassionate conservative
- Tax and spend liberal

I argue nearly half the electorate, based on their worldview, has already defined the candidate of its choice for the most part.

The point is that defining yourself is important.

But it's a bit more complicated for brand managers. Consumers are not blank slates marketers can simply stamp with brand messages until they are believed and bought.

Brands don't belong to companies.

Your organization might spend a lot of money sculpting its brand.

But it's not yours.

It resides in the mind of the consumer.

Which is why you alone cannot define yourself or your brand.

Co-creation of story and how to influence it will be addressed in the next section.

Remember though, it's revelation that gets you in the door and affords you a chance to influence co-creation. By revealing something unique you are helping your audience define you. You are steering it toward a favorable definition. You won't ever fully control that definition. But you can influence it.

Wrap your message in revelation.

Your audience will discover the truth for itself.

PURPOSEFUL REVELATION

What you choose to reveal isn't likely to be random.

The revelation you select should be aligned with your business objective.

A random revelation that is not connected in some way with your objective is not likely to produce the result you desire.

- Identify your objective
- Understand the worldview at stake
- Connect revelation with worldview

Choosing an appropriate revelation is an art.

It's personal.

And choosing correctly depends on the story your audience is telling itself. Just commit to being audience-centric.

Let it guide you.

Listen actively and those you wish to influence will identify the value at stake.

LET'S FIGHT

Without conflict you have no story.

Without a conflict-rich story your effort will not be believable. If your story isn't believable it's not likely to spread. If you've created an unbelievable story that lacks the ability to spread then it's not worthy of the time, effort, and money spent.

Conflict is the basis for revelation.

For instance, the musher who guides his sled dogs to a win at the Iditarod is not the story. The conflict the team overcomes is the story:

- The bloody paw the lead dog injured on Day 1 but kept going
- The seemingly impossible sled repair made using a dog collar
- The storm the musher shielded his dogs from by covering them with his jacket

Likewise, the executive who receives a promotion is not the story. The conflict the executive overcame is the story:

- How this executive was abandoned at a firehouse by her mother as a baby
- How she was repeatedly discriminated against in a male-dominated profession
- How she started her own company to prove herself before climbing the ladder

You're correct.

I'm making up these stories.

But these types of stories exist underneath the masks people, places, and processes wear. In fact, my experience as a news reporter is that the real stories are often more compelling than anything a fiction writer could dream up.

But often people don't recognize the story within.

Or they're afraid to tell it.

Publicly recognizing conflict can be uncomfortable for those not used to it. Conventional wisdom says we should ignore, minimize, or omit it from the stories we tell. But when we delete conflict from our story we also gut it of the very thing that makes it a story.

You must engage conflict if you want to engage an audience.

Conflict is the villain we need to reveal ourselves to those we wish to influence in a credible way. Without a villain to reveal our true character, we are simply clean storytellers shouting at the world about how great we are but without proof.

Overcoming conflict provides the proof an audience requires.

It's how we show listeners we are different rather than telling them and hoping they believe us.

Professional fighter Chael Sonnen once wore a t-shirt to the octagon where men fight one another that read, "Everyday I Fight."

It's true of everyone.

Not just professional fighters.

Dirty Storytelling

The great thing about conflict is that it's relative. It can be different and personal for everyone experiencing it. Or not.

Conflict lies in the eye of the conflicted.

A storyteller can illustrate conflict on three levels:

1. Inner Conflict
2. Interpersonal Conflict
3. Extra-personal Conflict

Inner Conflict

Inner conflict is the type had with oneself. It is characterized by the cognitive distress that accompanies irreconcilable choices. A protagonist experiencing inner conflict is forced to make choices that conflict with one another. The choices made often resolve one conflict but amplify another. Inner conflict may be experienced both consciously and subconsciously.

Interpersonal Conflict

Interpersonal conflict is the type had between two people. It is characterized by the incompatible desires of protagonists and antagonists. The choices made during interpersonal conflict serve either to attain one's desires or prevent another from attaining their desire.

Extra-personal Conflict

Extra-personal conflict is the type had between a person and something of which is not human. It is characterized as a struggle between the competing desires of man vs. nature, the earth, society, government, religion, fate, technology etc.

Dilemma is at the core of each level of conflict.
 Dilemma is the choice we must make between either the lesser of two evils or the greater of two goods.
 You're familiar with dilemma as it has prompted a number of clichés:

- Catch-22 situation
- Damned if you do, damned if you don't
- Caught between a rock and a hard place

We've been taught conflict is bad, destructive, and something to be avoided.
 It may be in some cases.
 But conflict is natural. It is a fact of life. And it is omnipresent.
 Life cannot be lived conflict-free. The honest will acknowledge they are, to a degree, in a constant state of conflict. They also attempt to view the state of constant conflict in which they find themselves as an opportunity for growth.
 Stripping conflict from story is not realistic or believable.
 Find the conflict, or mud, in your story.

SEVEN PLACES TO FIND MUD

We all have mud to sling.

But seeing our own mud can be difficult in a world where we have learned to hide our imperfections, mistakes, and blemishes. Clean storytellers might find this especially difficult since they routinely scrub their stories of conflict, or dirt, and aren't used to including it in story.

The key is training yourself to see the story in your dirt. Here are seven places to find or start seeing the dirt you'll need to tell stories that are believable and spreadable.

1. SLIT YOUR WRISTS

Cut deep into your fears, failures, and foolishness to find the dirt you need to create a compelling story. One reason some are frightened to *mudstorm*, the dirty storyteller's version of brainstorming, for imperfection is because they believe their shortcomings are unique. As a television news reporter I routinely heard the victims of tragedy, crime, and personal strife tell me, "You don't know what I've been through." They were certain I wasn't capable of understanding the horrible situations in which they found themselves. Victims feel extremely lonely. They often feel as if they are the only ones who have ever been through the situation in which they find themselves. In reality, victims are not alone and it's relatively easy to understand exactly through what people in turmoil are going. Victims are unique but their situations are not. While the details will vary most of us have experienced situations or emotions very similar to those experienced by victims. Victims are not alone. They are actually joining a crowded club of empathetic and understanding peers who understand more deeply than victims initially suspect. Keep this in mind when mudstorming for revelations. You aren't alone. You aren't the only one who has goofed up, forgotten something, or missed their target. However, you will be unique if you're courageous enough to show the world how you reacted to a challenge and what it can learn from you. The deeper you go the more compelling your revelation.

II. LOOK BEHIND YOU

It's easy to become fixated on that which is in front of us. The present is busy and we often perceive the future as even busier. These are reasons so many of us forget to turn around and look behind us. We must discipline ourselves to look over our shoulders. We've had this notion pounded out of us by self-help gurus and coaches who tell us to forget about the past. But there is often gold we never see sitting right behind us. I learned early on as a news reporter the real story was often behind me. What's in front of us is often manufactured to distract us while someone gets away with something behind our backs. It's similar to the discipline sharp arson investigators develop. The crackling flames, screaming victims, and sirens are all right there in front of the investigators. But the good investigators look behind them because they know arsonists sometimes return to the scene, keep a low profile, and watch their work from a distance. Train yourself to turn around. The dirt is often behind you.

III. REVERSE ENGINEER YOUR DIRT

I often urge people to be successful backward or to reverse engineer their success. You can also find mud to sling by working backward. Start by narrowly identifying what change you want to cause in your target audience. In other words, what do you want them to do that they aren't doing now? Continue working backward through *The Dirty Storytelling Model* by answering the questions in the worksheets scattered throughout the book and on **dirtystorytelling.com**. Working backward will often lead you directly to the type of revelation or metaphor you need to kick off your story. When it does, cut deep and key in on the imperfection you believe is most likely to connect.

IV. METAPHOR

Researchers estimate we use several metaphors every minute we speak. Metaphors are key components of memory. Metaphors are how we connect the dots, interpret the complex, and frame the abstract. Metaphors are shortcuts to connections that count. It's why I hope you'll consider converting your revelation to metaphor when appropriate. Don't use metaphor in place of riveting detail. However, we provide our audiences shortcuts for comprehending and connecting with us emotionally when we reveal through metaphor.

V. TINY MOMENTS

Think small when searching for revelations to introduce. An ounce of detail is worth more than a pound of context, at least initially. Focus on a brief moment in time, the tiniest of details, or a small sliver of the overall scene. Describe this moment in great detail. Do so after reliving, imagining, or empathetically gaining an appreciation for the value at stake in this brief moment of time. The tiny details about your revelations are memorable and may be revisited at the ends of your stories. Don't feel pressured to set a broad scene at the outset. There'll be plenty of time for that later. The more granular you can get at the outset the bigger your hook. And even great stories are ignored if they don't immediately hook their audiences. Do it with detail.

VI. AGILITY & ANGLES

If you find yourself struggling in respect to finding new mud to sling stop searching and start investigating. By new mud I mean revelations or tops to stories that haven't been told the way you'll tell them. If you're concerned your revelation or story has already been told by someone else, that doesn't mean you can't do it differently. Your angle, or the trail you cut to your story, can prompt an audience to perceive a lesson they have heard hundreds of times as unique and well told. When you get stumped, and you will, read, listen, and explore what has already been done. Consume everything that has already been said, written, or pantomimed on the topic. Then ask yourself what aspect, perspective, or question has not been explored. Identifying what hasn't been done is your entry point and a basis for the angle that'll make your rendition of the story unique. Likewise, being mentally agile will help you spot external opportunities to tell dirty stories. Mental agility, in part, is a marketer's ability to look at headlines, conventional wisdom, or current events and use them to mentally pivot and cause others to see these items differently than they had previously. Challenge the status quo, ask why, or show why the conventional wisdom on display is wrong. Storytellers constantly on the prowl for material will quickly begin to see opportunities to interrupt the status quo with revelations that uniquely position them as thought leaders.

VII. GAWK AT GAPS

Gaps between expectation and reality are where storytellers find treasure. I'll discuss gaps and how to use them in greater detail later. But it's important to begin noticing gaps now and why they're so valuable to storytellers. Gaps provide storytellers with all sorts of revelations. Gaps provide the plots for movies, situation comedies, and comedic routines. Realities that are out of sync with expectations provide the conflict a hero needs to begin her quest. Gaps that widen as story progresses allow antagonists to enter and create the potential for deeper audience participation. Start noticing gaps between expectation and reality. Gawk at these gaps. Then look inward, deeply, and backward at the gaps you have encountered and the revelations they provide.

START SLINGING MUD WORKSHEET

The questions in each section are aimed at helping you probe your organization, product, or service in a manner that identifies, categorizes, and prioritizes revelations potentially useful in achieving your marketing goals.

I. IDENTIFY THE MUD

Start by mudstorming or listing the obstacles, challenges, or hurdles that come to mind when answering the following questions.

1. List the challenges that caused you to lose sleep, check your email late at night, or work on weekends to overcome recently. Why weren't the issues resolved earlier? What behavior won't you repeat? What behavior will you insist upon in the future?

2. Name three things you expected to execute easily but wound up being more difficult than anticipated? What surprised you? How could you have prepared differently for the project or anticipated the surprise another way?

3. Identify a project of which you were initially skeptical but that wound up succeeding. Why was your skepticism founded or unfounded? Identify a project of which you were initially confident but that wound up failing. Why was your confidence founded or unfounded?

4. What would cause you to go out of business in 5, 10, or 20 years? Of the factors you identify, over which do you have some degree of control? What do you see as your organization or industry's biggest blind spot, liability, or assumption?

II. CATEGORIZE THE MUD

Build upon the answers you provided in section one by categorizing them according to their level of conflict. Beneath each level of conflict are additional questions aimed at narrowing your focus.

1. **Inner Conflict**- When last did you doubt yourself and why? Which choices caused you to be torn between the lesser of two evils or the greater of two goods? How specifically did you resolve your doubt or dilemma?

2. **Interpersonal Conflict**- When last were you torn in response to a customer service issue? Why was the situation unique & what criteria did you use to resolve it? What type of issues have you encountered with a competitor? Did you respond directly to the competitor or resolve the matter by communicating directly with your customers? Why? Which employee issue have you found to be the most challenging, counterintuitive, or surprising? Are there surefire solutions that have failed to resolve the issue or unexpected fixes that have been particularly effective?

3. **Extra-personal Conflict**- Which ideas or technologies have the greatest potential to disrupt your organization or industry? Who is pioneering or advancing these ideas and technologies and how soon might they begin bearing fruit? How might future legislation, regulation, and litigation cause you to alter your strategy? What kinds of shifts in culture, social norms, or societal values have the greatest potential to change customer behavior?

III. PRIORITIZE THE MUD

This section will help you align the potential revelations you've identified with pertinent business objectives. You may recognize a pattern in regard to which category of conflict your potential revelations fall. If so, it may allow you to structure a series of communications aimed at exploiting your expertise in those areas.

1. **Rank the Dirt**- list the 3-5 revelations you believe would be most damaging should they be made public and list why that might be.

2. **Flip the Dirt**- now flip each revelation and position your organization as having solved the problem, jumped the hurdle, or overcome the challenge. Example) Revelation: None of my students read the eBooks we bought. Flip: The secret (my organization) uncovered that'll get your students to read the eBooks you bought.

3. **Re-rank the Dirt**- now rank the flips based on what you believe would be most beneficial to your organization and valuable to your audience should they be made public.

4. **Objectives**- list some of your business communications or marketing goals.

5. **Match Dirt with Objective-** match the flips you just created with the goals you feel they'll help you achieve. If none of the flips appear to be congruent with your objectives, revisit your list of potential revelations.

Visit www.dirtystorytelling.com to download free copies of this worksheet and new *Dirty Storytelling* resources.

Nick Winkler

SLING MUD TOGETHER

Story belongs not to you but to them. Only after you earn their attention might you be afforded an opportunity to influence the story they tell about you.

THE DIRTY FUTURE

I had prepared for a fight, a chase, and the possibility of being tossed into a Native American jail with none of the rights I would have on nontribal land.

As an investigative television news reporter I had run through every scenario I could possibly imagine prior to confronting a city official who we had caught repeatedly gambling in a tribal casino while he was being paid by taxpayers to work.

As was the case in many of the confrontations I initiated, my predictions of how the casino confrontation would turn out were wrong.

We found our guy, he painfully answered our questions, and we got out of there before security could handcuff and haul us to jail.

While it didn't turn out the way I anticipated it did not keep me from continuing to tell myself stories about the future.

I'm certainly not alone in this predictive endeavor.

We are wired to wonder.

Right now our prospects and customers are telling themselves stories about the future. Will you stand idly by and allow these stories to be told without you? Or will you try to influence the story they're telling?

You don't have a choice if you want to remain in business.

Rather than ignoring the stories prospects are telling about the future like clean storytellers do, smart marketers look for ways to help prospects tell their stories. Savvy storytellers look for ways to influence the story they know will be told with or without them.

There's a seat at the storytelling table waiting for you. Will you take your seat?

PARTNERS IN STORY

When you understand story, at least the kind people believe, will be created with or without you, your job as a marketer becomes much clearer.

You can't create believable story in a silo anymore.

If you try to overpower people with clean story you'll likely fail or run out of money trying.

The strategy now is to partner with your audience in the co-creation of story.

Co-creation is difficult for some to get their hands around. Some might envision a chess match in which opposing storytellers are trying to outfox one another and react intelligently until a winner is crowned and a story is told.

Co-creation is not a competition.

If you treat it as a competitive game you'll lose. If you aggressively move to win the game you believe you're playing you'll lose even quicker. And if you bully your co-creator as if he were an adversary, he'll simply ignore you and there'll be nothing to win or co-create.

Instead, think of co-creation as mutually hosting an event.

One you both want to be successful and inspire people to talk about long after it's over. You'll do things that aren't your job. You'll engage in ways you hadn't expected. And you'll cover for your co-host without being asked.

You'll do all this not because you hope your co-host notices but because you want the event you're hosting to be a success.

Co-creation is about nuance, subtlety, and finesse.

Remember, in terms of *The Dirty Storytelling Model*, you've already hit your audience over the head with a massive revelation. You've surprised them, violated their expectations, or struck a counterintuitive nerve.

You have their attention.

Don't blow it with bluster.

Co-creation is a time to back off a bit.

Arouse, inspire, and lead softly.

DIRTY STORY MOTHERS

Stories are a bit like children.

People will often protect both at all costs.

Storytellers often believe the stories they tell themselves despite contradictory evidence. It's as if they conceived, birthed, and raised the story they hold dear like it was a child. Storytellers are like mothers protecting their children from a dangerous world.

Wouldn't it be great if we could get people to adopt our child, our story?

If so, they'd undoubtedly protect, nurture, and care for our story as if it were their own. We could rest easy that, should we ever have to give up our story, it would be in good hands.

In essence, this is the goal of co-creation.

Dirty Storytelling

The idea is to create an environment in which your audience helps create the proof by which it is convinced. An audience will take partial ownership in a story it discovers, connects with, and helps create.

The key is creating an environment in which this can happen.

Remember, subtlety is your friend.

Later, on page 126, I'll show you why what you leave out of a story is sometimes more important than what you put in.

But first, if we want people to spread our story in the future, we must first ensure they convince themselves it's worthy of spreading. Your job is to transform the marketing process into a shared experience that, at least for a time, your audience doesn't know it is sharing. If you can wrap your audience in a compelling story you'll no longer be marketing to them.

You'll be helping them along on a journey in which they discover for themselves why your idea is of value to them and why it's worth telling others about.

Giving up your child, your story, is frightening. The prospect of handing over story will prompt fear to creep in. Fear will try to convince you it's not worth it. That clean stories are a safer and wiser choice.

You'll crave message control. You'll purposefully forget that control is an illusion. You'll want to give in to your fear.

Full disclosure, the exact message you want the world to hear is not the one that'll come out at the end of the co-creation process. And it certainly won't be the one that remains intact should your story spread.

Remember, message perfection should no longer be your aim nor is it possible.

Believability is your goal.

So you have to let go.

Good mothers do let go but still manage to keep tabs, right?

If you are effective in helping your audience create the proof by which it is convinced the core of your message, the part that deserves to spread, will likely remain intact enough to prompt the change you desire.

The essence of your story will survive.

You are what you are but you're also what you are not. At times, what you are not is the story the audience will see and spread. The story is theirs to tell. Work hard at being subtle and guide your audience in the direction you prefer.

After that, the audience will choose a specific path.

That's what co-creation is about.

Without it you'll still have a story.

Just not one anyone cares enough about to spread.

DIRTY STORIES ARE UFOS (UNIDENTIFIED FEELING OBJECTS)

Dirty stories, or UFOs, abduct people.

They transport their captives on trips that arouse emotion in ways that prompt people to heed calls to action.

Dirty Storytelling

Afterward, when the UFO returns its captives, they're inspired to tell others about the trip, how it changed them, and why it matters.

Dirty stories are UFOs or *Unidentified Feeling Objects*. They change the way people feel. And they do so with permission.

UFOs touch, connect with, and move people. The insight that results from this emotion is what changes people. Don't underestimate a UFO though. While the storytellers who fly them understand they must first change how people feel before changing what they do, they know they must also include evidence.

So lost somewhere in story, amid all the emotion, is fact, data, or evidence. The storyteller understands he must deliver this but in a way that compels. If told well, story reveals its evidence as insight to a delighted audience.

Insight answers the question why.

"I just want to know why?"

That's the question I heard as a news reporter from crying mothers, victims of horrible tragedies, and even those who have cheated death. People are consumed with understanding why an event occurred.

The irony is we don't often immediately know. We must know what can't immediately be known.

So our thirst for learning why often takes us on a journey that results in answers but not true insight. We crave meaning and in the absence of fact we'll create our own. Amid great uncertainty we'll find clarity. None of it may be accurate but it's true to us.

If others cannot answer why for us, we'll answer it ourselves.

We do so to make sure the gruesome never happens again. Or with the hope we might replicate a miracle.

We create meaning when none exists.

We satisfy our thirst, our emotional craving to know why.

Story allows for this.

It's the emotional delivery of why.

INVEST IN EMOTION

Ever wonder why people often choose inferior products or services?

Your offering may include superior features, advantages, and benefits but consumers often buy from inferior competitors. In response, you tout your offering's value proposition even louder but still can't convince your target.

The problem isn't with your offering.

It's likely how you're touting it.

Instead of dissecting the inferior offering that's eating your lunch, inspect the story being told about the inferior offering. Chances are it's arousing emotion in consumers that changes how they feel about the offering.

Remember, the problem isn't likely with your offering.

The emotional decisions people make are often in conflict with how ration says they ought to behave. It's why financial traders often buy high and sell low. It's why auctions often fetch higher selling prices than other commercial transactions. It's why men pay a premium for diamonds that come in signature light blue boxes than those that do not.

Our emotions routinely guide our ration. This isn't to say logic doesn't play a key role in consumer preference and purchasing decisions. It simply means when emotion takes the steering wheel of our minds, ration has little choice but to sit in the back seat and wait for an opening to regain control.

As an investigative television news reporter, I routinely witnessed people make emotional decisions that put themselves at great personal risk:

- Whistleblowers who could lose their jobs should they be identified as the one who exposed the boss
- A tipster willing to trade an explosive secret for anonymity that, if blown, could result in tremendous personal harm
- A grieving mother who sets aside her fear of crying, being embarrassed, or saying something she wished she hadn't in an effort to prevent other children from meeting the same fate as her child

There is much at stake in each instance. From a logical standpoint, the risk of becoming a source clearly outweighs the reward to the whistleblower, tipster, or grieving mother. But logic is not on which their decisions are based.

Nick Winkler

Their decision to speak to me was based on emotion. A value is at stake in each case.

In journalism the value at stake is often justice.

A source's world has been knocked out of balance by injustice. The source, no longer able to stomach the injustice, sets out on a quest to restore justice and balance. Under pressure, the source makes decisions that carry tremendous personal risk. But it's worth the risk to restore justice and bring about change.

What value is at stake in your offering?

It doesn't have to be as dramatic or important as justice. But if there is nothing at stake in the minds of your prospects how will your offering help them achieve what they hope to by being in the market for offerings like yours?

Remember, they are on a quest.

If your offering is void of emotion, what will compel them to choose it as a tool that helps them restore balance in their lives?

To be the crusaders they see themselves as.

YOU'RE A CAPE

Not a superhero.

Your offering, no matter how much better it is than a competitor's, is nothing more than a cape that helps your superhero customer take flight.

Ego, narcissism, and arrogance trick us into thinking otherwise. But the truth is our offerings are simply means to ends for those who use them.

111

Dirty Storytelling

Watch commercials made by car manufacturers, drug makers, and household cleaning product makers. They depict customers overcoming, overachieving, or over delivering with the help of the products, not because of them.

The car helps the baby boomer reclaim youth.

The drug helps the patient heal himself.

The cleaning product helps the user protect her family.

Disciplined storytellers constantly remind themselves the customer is the hero in the story being told.

Here is your cape hero.

Now fly!

YOU GOT BAD ADVICE

About injecting emotion into your stories.

Marketers who believe they're in charge of emotion have been misled.

You can't inject, cause, or force people to experience emotion.

But you can arouse it.

Your job is to lay a foundation that creates an environment in which emotion can be aroused in an audience.

Pleasure and pain are the only two emotions.

Variations exist.

But smart marketers choose one as a basis from which to work.

ALERT: Just because you sell a commodity, are a manufacturer, or are otherwise engaged in the blue collar creation of hard assets does not mean emotion isn't important to your success.

What I'm telling you is rooted in evolution and psychology.

Here's a scenario to consider; an early ancestor confronts a hungry predator. Fight or flight kicks in. Ancestor escapes with a memory of the encounter that reminds him to steer clear of the predator in the future, thus helping him and his family to survive.

We're all here, some argue, thanks to that memory.

Why did the ancestor remember this particular encounter? He remembered, in part, because he was stressed. The stress that causes our fight or flight reaction stamps our memory.

Emotional experiences are simply more likely to be remembered.

James L. McGaugh, a human memory researcher, is responsible for this insight which anyone who cares about their brand should understand.

In essence, McGaugh found our brains have evolved to remember emotionally arousing experiences. Stress is a type of emotional arousal and stimulates the portion of the brain responsible for memory creation.

We stress.

We remember.

Now consider psychologist Jerome Bruner's estimate that a fact is 20 times more likely to be remembered if it's part of a story.

It means a well told story that arouses an emotional reaction is likely to be remembered.

- If you manufacture vehicle brake pads, then you sell family safety rather than brakes
- If you're in the business of chrome plating metal, you're selling polished beauty rather than chemicals
- And if you raise livestock for a living, you're selling a way of life rather than cattle

Okay, ready to arouse emotion?
  Roll up your pant legs then.
  You're gonna get dirty.

YOU'RE ONLY AS GOOD AS YOUR DIRT

I've been picking fights my entire life.
  As an investigative television news reporter I picked fights with the powerful, the pitiful, and the phony. I waged war against corruption, waste, and inefficiency. Even in the midst of one fight, I was already lining up my next.
  I craved a bigger, tougher, more vicious opponent each fight I fought.
  Why?
  The more anger or disdain my viewers had for my opponent, the more they were likely to love me. This is how you create compelling stories. This is how you get an audience to fall in love with a protagonist.
  It's the only way to inspire change.

You line up the bad guys, build an army of support, and work together to keep the bad guys from hurting you.

I understood I could not fully develop myself or my news station as protagonists unless I found and confronted memorable antagonists. The more heinous, despised, or insurmountable the villain, the greater the odds were that viewers would root for me.

I wanted to inspire change.

I wanted our viewers to watch our newscast more frequently. I wanted viewers of other newscasts to switch to my newscast. And I wanted everyone who witnessed the antagonism to rally for change that restored the imbalance antagonists had created.

It's counterintuitive.

Clean storytellers do not understand it's the antagonist that makes a story emotionally compelling. The bad guy is the one who prompts an audience to care and root for the good guy. Without the bad guy, a good gal's true character will never be revealed on a deep level.

Why?

We're lazy. Others would say efficient. Either way, we don't generally expend any more energy than we must to achieve our goals. In other words, we don't like to risk anything unless we have to.

We need to be pushed.

It's the forces of antagonism that require more of us. It's the villain that motivates us to step up. Without antagonism we're left with no real reason to care about the protagonist.

Want people to invest emotionally in your story? Then develop the antagonists in great detail.

Develop complex antagonists so strong there's no doubt they have the power to inflict pain, suffering, and agony on your audience. This is what causes an audience to change. People buy products, switch brands, or try new products to prevent the antagonist from having its way with them:

- Old age or the loss of youth are the antagonists sports car makers use to change baby boomers
- Embarrassment or inadequacy are the antagonists home cleaning product makers use to change homemakers
- Being ignorant, passed over, or poor are the antagonists authors, trainers, and coaches use to change middle managers looking to get ahead

When storytellers develop powerful antagonists audiences often feel they have no choice but to act to stop the antagonist from crushing them. It's the forces of antagonism that cause them to buy what you're selling.

Stories well told are this powerful.

It's also why they're dangerous in the wrong hands.

BEHIND THE DIRTY CURTAIN

That's where I'm asking you to follow me now.

Behind the curtain of this book you'll find the mechanics of story. You are the protagonist who has set out on a quest to make your marketing more effective. Powerful antagonists such as clean stories, fear, and the desire to hide your faults are working to prevent you from achieving your goal.

But if I have done a good job describing the antagonists, or the marketing death you'll endure and the havoc the antagonists will wreak if left unchecked, you'll change. You'll stop sanitizing your story. You'll start telling dirty stories as part of your marketing. You'll restore the balance you've lost.

You'll save your marketing life.

My point in taking you behind the curtain is not just to illustrate story, identify the parts, and transparently show how they fit together. It's to highlight the responsibility a storyteller has to her audience.

No doubt you've been burned by a storyteller.

We all have.

The kind that whip us into frenzies, promise us a fix, and sell us something that does not fulfill the promise made.

These kinds of storytellers get a lot of attention because their solutions don't actually solve the problem they promise to solve. In instances like these, we often complain the product or service doesn't work.

We're often mistaken though.

Dirty Storytelling

It's relatively easy to make things today. The majority of things work. They just don't work in ways that meet our expectations.

The problem is not the product it's the antagonist.

The villain created to sell many products and services is so powerful nothing is truly sufficient to stop it. Unscrupulous storytellers regrettably get carried away in terms of developing antagonists.

We have a responsibility as storytellers to be honest about forces of antagonism. Exaggerating, embellishing, or inventing antagonists often backfires and pushes customers away. It erases trust and ensures a story about you will spread. Just not one of which you'll be proud.

Our audiences will hold us accountable if we do not do so ourselves.

As a reporter I only picked fights with those who deserved to be exposed. I only fought people who behaved egregiously. My focus was on people whose behavior was unquestionably wrong.

Were I to behave otherwise people would likely stop watching my newscast and I would have eventually found myself involuntarily out of work as a reporter.

Authentic antagonists are the only kind about which you should tell stories. Resist the urge to manipulate by creating straw men. Refrain from selling by exaggerating the threat or consequences. You don't need to invent forces of antagonism.

Genuine villains are aplenty.

Just like clean stories.

Nick Winkler

VILLAINS ARE LIKE ICE CREAM

Now that we've had our ethics reminder, I'd like you to mudstorm for potential antagonists in your stories. Hunt for and line them up. Pile on the forces of antagonism as if they were ice cream toppings.

The more the merrier.

We find out who we really are on the battlefield not when we're visiting Disneyland. We must actively seek out those who'll test us. Only by performing under increasing amounts of pressure will you prompt change.

Remember, the more trouble you find the more memorable the Saturday night!

But antagonism isn't only about quantity. The quality, or complexity of the forces of antagonism, is often what prompts change.

It's why a little boy from a bad neighborhood is a hero of mine.

I met Carlos, a charmingly humble 9-year-old who was mature beyond his years, as a television news reporter covering the burglary that left him and his family without Christmas presents. It was a routine smash and grab. Had the thieves been the only antagonists involved, newscast viewers would never have been inspired to help right the wrong.

Viewers fell in love with Carlos.

Carlos was the only English speaker in his home. He translated for his parents, helped them with their banking, and made sure they responded to the mail they received.

Dirty Storytelling

Carlos was also responsible for his younger siblings. He walked them to school, kept them away from the gangs trying to recruit them, and made sure they had something to eat at night.

Carlos was the little man of the house.

He was on his own though after the burglary. The police weren't going to devote the manpower necessary to identify the burglars who stole his family's Christmas.

Initially, Carlos turned down my request for an interview. He was too busy asking neighbors if they had any odd jobs for him. Just days before Christmas, and Carlos was trying to earn enough money to replace the presents stolen from his younger siblings.

Carlos did finally grant me an interview. When I asked whether he knew he was different from other 9-year-olds he told me in a faint Spanish accent, "I am just trying to make good decisions for my family."

Do you feel what the viewers felt?

It's as if they were saying, "How could these bastards do this to my adorable Carlos?"

- The burglars
- The bad neighborhood
- The gangs
- The inattentive police
- The language barrier
- The oversized responsibility
- The chores
- The unfairness

- The stolen Christmas

The people who heard this story reacted the only way their consciences would allow—with generosity. Viewers bought gifts, delivered them to Carlos, and asked only for hugs in return.

Viewers had fallen in love with Carlos. His story changed them. They interrupted their regular holiday routines, bought gifts for strangers, and delivered them to a little boy in a rough neighborhood they otherwise would never have visited.

Carlos reacted to life courageously.

That's why Oklahoma City fell in love with him.

But it never would've happened without the antagonists.

REACTION IS STORY

There'd be no Superman without conflict.

Clark Kent's transformation depends upon forces of antagonism. Without crises, obstacles, or challenges Kent would never have a reason to turn into Superman. Without antagonists there'd be nothing to save, no one to rescue, and nothing compelling about which an audience should care.

Anyone who loves Superman, or any hero for that matter, owes a debt of gratitude to the bad guys responsible for revealing a hero's true character.

While antagonists may be the ladders we use to climb to the top of story, they are not the story. Story is the reaction to antagonism. Understanding and believing this is the key to managing the fear you'll encounter when considering whether to tell dirty stories.

The fear of revealing an imperfection, acknowledging a stumble, or publicly discussing forces of antagonism often cause marketers to play it safe by telling clean stories. What clean storytellers miss is that imperfection, stumbles, and antagonists are not the story. Your reaction to these foes is story.

- Story is Reggie Jackson's heroic three home run performance to win the World Series, not his off the field controversy
- Story is Oprah Winfrey overcoming adversity to build a media empire, not the poverty, abuse, or criticism
- Story is Carlos, a child rising to meet adult-like challenges, not the Christmas burglars, gangs, or bad neighborhood

Antagonists allow us a chance to win the hearts of an audience. It's our reaction to adversity and the challenges that follow that determine whether we connect with those we wish to influence.

Initial reactions are telling. But subsequent reaction, the increasingly difficult choices made under increasingly intense pressure, are the ones that coax the co-creation of story.

The greater the insight revealed, the more an audience invests emotionally. An audience that begins to anticipate, wonder, and worry about what's next is one that has a stake in the story being told.

The audience is actively engaged in the telling as well.

But where does a protagonist meet the challenges that create this bond?

The gap between expectation and reality is where story resides. The gap is the distance between a protagonist and his desire.

Without a gap there is no story.

The bigger the gap—the more compelling the story. Your job as a dirty storyteller is to identify these gaps, pry them open, and allow the antagonists to flood the gap in an effort to keep the desire from being fulfilled.

For example, it's not news if someone is killed by a drunk driver on a Saturday night. It is news if I interview a man who admits he has been driving drunk for 69 years, has never been stopped, and plans on continuing to do so until he eventually kills someone.

This is news because the gap between expectation and reality is so great.

It's not news if a thief steals something and goes to jail. It is news if a thief steals something, feels guilty as he is getting away, and returns to the store to apologize to the manager and return the item. Again, the gap between expectation and reality here is great.

Clean stories are gap-free.

They deliver to the consumer exactly what the consumer has come to expect:

- Marketing brochures that tout your product as bigger, better, or faster
- News releases hyping mundane corporate happenings
- Sales pitches that falsely warn time is running out

These aren't stories that compel people to act.

What you're delivering with clean stories is exactly what the consumer expects. It's why clean stories are so easy to ignore.

When we receive exactly what we expect we quickly tune it out. We shift our attention to matters that surprise us. When we are surprised we devote more of ourselves to the surprise.

We are wired to notice the atypical.

Gaps offer the storyteller opportunities to surprise.

A gap is often created when an antagonist prevents the protagonist from getting what he wants. This forces the protagonist to react. Doing so prompts greater antagonism which cracks the gap open even wider. Now the protagonist is forced to make increasingly risky choices to achieve his desire.

The reaction is what matters to your audience.

Revealing imperfection can be scary.

I won't tell you otherwise. But I'll also tell you that feeling fear means you're getting closer to what you want. *Dirty Storytelling Hall of Famer* Steven Pressfield says expect fear to increase the closer you get.

Your job isn't to eliminate fear but manage it.

When you do you'll earn an opportunity to co-create story with the people who are important to you.

DIRTY REWARDS

Your audience is rewarded when you tell dirty stories with it.

Dirty stories create environments that compel audiences to wonder what's next, invest emotionally, and take an ownership stake in the outcome. The audience helps create the proof by which it is convinced and is then inspired to tell others about it.

The audience gains insight from the co-created story.

If constructed properly, the insight co-created story produces is valuable to its co-creators. When it's valuable your audience will take great pride in telling others.

It'll be a gift worth giving.

People who are compelled to co-create story that changes them find pleasure in passing that creation to others who they believe will benefit.

The story that convinced them may also convince those they tell.

Co-creation is a foundation for stories that spread by word of mouth.

When you invest in co-creation you increase the odds others will share the story made. In addition to the ideas outlined thus far, the following ten techniques will help you create an environment that stimulates co-creation and belief.

TEN WAYS TO CO-CREATE STORY
Help Your Audience Create the Proof by Which It's Convinced

I. CREATE HOLES

The details you leave out of your story are often as important as those you choose to include. Storytellers can earn and keep attention by intentionally withholding information from listeners. Leaving holes throughout your story allows an audience to internalize the story. Listeners will fill the holes you leave. They'll create pieces of the story you leave blank. Songwriters know this well. It's why the best, when asked what a particularly ambiguous song means, never answer thoroughly. Were they to do so they'd ruin the song for those who have developed their own interpretation of the song. Guy Clark, a songwriter from Texas and *Dirty Storytelling Hall of Famer*, says to create an opportunity for people to relate or associate with songs, "You have to leave holes in the right places. You can't detail everything perfectly or they (listeners) have no room to get inside it or to allow it to touch them." So give them some room to get in and leave their mark. Scatter your holes strategically. Ask yourself of what you want the audience to convince itself. Lead it to that conclusion with detail you provide. Then leave a hole it can fill.

II. STRATEGIC SILENCE

Insert silence when you are interested in making a particular detail memorable. Silence may be inserted after a key detail you provide or a hole you leave for the audience to fill. People confronted with silence in interpersonal situations often find themselves uncomfortable with it. To alleviate the discomfort silence can cause, people often fill the silence. For instance, investigative reporters will often stare blankly at an interview subject and say nothing. The majority of interviewees are not savvy enough to identify what's happening and begin talking to fill the uncomfortable silence. In doing so, they often reveal information that would not have otherwise been revealed. But silence isn't necessarily staring at someone sitting across from you. Silence takes whatever form it must to conform to the media or platform in which it is inserted. Inserting silence lets a story breathe and often prompts listeners to consider the preceding detail on a deeper level. Use silence for emphasis. Is there a particularly complex idea in your story that may require additional thought? Is there a particular idea, symbol, or phrase you want to illuminate without words? Silence is your spotlight. Build in silence so listeners will fill it with their words, attention, thoughts, and deeds.

III. MAKE U-TURNS

Since we know people pay extra attention to surprises it makes sense not only to surprise them, but also to amplify those surprises. We'll get a better return on our surprise if we set it up appropriately. Screenwriters often dramatically reverse the expectations of an audience when executing surprise plot twists. Business communicators will have less latitude in that they will not want an audience to feel as if it had been tricked, duped, or manipulated into paying attention. However, inserting miniature U-Turns in your story will amplify the surprise awaiting the audience. Simply identify what you want the audience to feel after it is surprised and emphasize the opposite prior to the surprise. Setting up a surprise in this manner enables it to deliver a bigger payoff. This is effective when challenging norms, violating expectations, and when you're aiming to be counterintuitive.

IV. RECRUIT STORY DETECTIVES

Prompt your audience to be curious by turning them into detectives. Reveal just enough after building intrigue so your audience will begin trying to figure out the ending on its own. This is how television news magazine shows like *48 Hours* and *Dateline* keep viewers engaged for a full hour. Create intrigue, provide detail, and tempt viewers into becoming detectives. When listeners become story detectives they make predictions about the future. Their curiosity builds as they compare these predictions with revelations you scatter throughout story. Once a listener begins to envision a story's outcome, they become emotionally invested in seeing how it unfolds.

Create a mystery, look for opportunities to prompt curiosity, and empower listeners to solve the mystery themselves.

V. BE AN IMAGINATION TRAINER

Your job as a storyteller is to be a trainer to your audience's imagination. We hire trainers to push us to the limit during gym workouts. A storyteller must do the same for an audience's imagination. Push it to the mental limit. Story must prompt those you wish to influence to ask, "What's next?" and "Why?" You can prompt listeners to ask these questions by including conflict in your stories. Only after there is conflict can an audience become empathetic. Empathy causes audiences to wonder about the outcome and to become emotionally invested in the story. An audience that begins to wonder about a story's outcome is more likely to stick around for it. Audiences that are rewarded for anticipating the future are more likely to be motivated to share the story.

VI. THE SECRET REVEAL

Reward your audience for anticipating, imagining, & co-creating story by revealing secrets throughout the journey. Secrets are treasures. They are pieces of insight for which an engaged audience craves. Insight is how an audience determines whether it is doing good detective work, correctly anticipating what's next, or imagining a future that's congruent with the story being told. If so, an audience will pat itself on the back and continue imagining. If not, you're giving the audience the insight necessary to recalibrate its imagined scenarios.

VII. THE RED DIRT DRIP

Red dirt musicians, those who play for audiences in Texas and Oklahoma, rarely begin on time. The artist is often late to the stage. This is by design. Not only does it give the dancehall a chance to sell more beer, it builds suspense and requires concertgoers to wait for their reward. The reward becomes more valuable when more is required to earn it. It's similar to the way storytellers must reward audiences; not too early and not all at once. When rewarding an audience, provide only the detail necessary to deliver the reward and prompt further engagement. In other words, storytellers interested in stimulating curiosity should cause their audiences wait. Withhold information until it is needed to continue imagining and co-creating.

VIII. THE COMEDIC GIFT OF MISTAKE

Revelations of imperfection can often be delivered comedically to spur the co-creation of story. Mistakes can be gifts if managed intelligently. Without mistakes, there'd be no Jerry Seinfeld, Bill Cosby, or Johnny Carson. When you poke fun at yourself publicly, you knock down a barrier that exists between you and your prospects. You humanize your organization and communicate a confidence words cannot. The great part about comedy is you know immediately whether it worked. Your audience laughs or it doesn't. Laughter is co-creation in its rawest and most obvious form. It's also rare since the majority is uncomfortable poking fun at the brands on which organizations have spent fortunes getting people to take seriously. However, framing a revelation of imperfection with humor will endear your organization to forgiving audiences that are often appreciative of laughter and the honesty it takes to cause it.

IX. WORDS NOT NECESSARY

Telling a story nonverbally is a surefire way to stimulate co-creation and help the audience create the proof by which it's convinced. For instance, television news directors used to tell nonverbal stories to get first time job seekers to accept meager salary offers. News directors would keep stacks of VHS reporter audition tapes in their offices just so candidates would see and be intimidated by the stacks during interviews. The stacks were nonverbal indicators of how much demand there was for a reporting job; hundreds of tapes for just one opening. There's no telling how many nervous young reporter candidates saw these stacks and said to themselves, "I had better take whatever salary is offered since there's so much competition for this job." Sometimes saying nothing is more powerful than any of the words you have at your disposal. Nonverbal storytelling is co-creation at its finest.

X. FOG THE CLARITY

Fogging the message is a technique politicians use to create ambiguity in support of less than noble intentions. Fogging a message politically means not being clear, precise, or specific in an effort to avoid being pinned down on a position or issue. Ultimately, storytellers want clarity in terms of their calls to action and an audience's response to them. However, immediate clarity isn't always preferred. Weaving a bit of ambiguity into story can stir an audience's imagination. Creating ambiguity signals to your audience it has permission to imagine. An imaginative audience is one that is more engaged and willing to invest in the co-creation of story. Look for opportunities where ambiguity can add to the substance of story. Invite your audience to imaginatively add the clarity you have purposefully left out. Fog the message to co-create story.

STORY CO-CREATION WORKSHEET

The questions or exercises beneath each co-creation technique will help you create an environment in which your audience helps create the proof by which it is convinced.

I. CREATE HOLES

1. List the key ideas you want your audience to conclude or discover for itself.

2. Work backward from each idea and identify the details you would have to supply for an audience to come to these conclusions on its own. Afterward, delete the conclusion, leave only the preceding detail necessary, and you've created mini-cliffhangers for your audience.

II. STRATEGIC SILENCE

1. List the ideas or details you wish to emphasize or spotlight. They may be complex ideas, comedic moments, or clues about an outcome.

2. Inserting silence after an idea you want to emphasize can impact the pacing of your story. Does the idea being emphasized call for immediate reaction? If so, do not insert silence. If not, use the medium on which you're working to identify what form silence may take.

III. MAKE U-TURNS

1. List the surprises you suspect will arouse emotion. What do you want your audience to feel when surprised? Work backward and identify details prior to the surprise that arouse the opposite emotion.

IV. RECRUIT STORY DETECTIVES

1. What's intriguing or mysterious about the problem you wish to help your audience solve?

2. How might you flip your offering's features, advantages, or benefits into clues or details that hint at the solution?

V. BE AN IMAGINATION TRAINER

1. Identify the idea or matter about which you want your audience to anticipate or wonder. What conflict could you insert prior to this idea or matter that would jeopardize or call it into question?

VI. THE SECRET REVEAL

1. What type of insight might you reveal that confirms or denies your audience is co-creating as you wish? Look for ways to reinforce, violate norms, or challenge the status quo.

VII. THE RED DIRT DRIP

1. Is there room in your story for mini-climaxes? Places you can heighten what's at stake but then quickly back away from?

2. Can you identify spots where silence or nonverbal communication can stretch and audience's imagination, prompt it to see prior events differently, or otherwise create additional anticipation for the ultimate resolution?

VIII. THE COMEDIC GIFT OF MISTAKE

1. Identify unflattering worldviews your prospects or customers hold. Which lend themselves to humor and how?

2. What role might comedy play in highlighting how an unflattering perception has been addressed or overcome?

IX. WORDS NOT NECESSARY

1. Identify how you want people to feel. List the design, packaging, or layout characteristics that can accomplish this in place of words.

X. FOG THE CLARITY

1. List the details you've included prior to surprises, before silence, or to stimulate imagination. Which, if any, are not vital for comprehension? How might you blur or create ambiguity with symbols, words, or silence?

Nick Winkler

TRIGGER A MUDSLIDE

Embed easy to pull triggers that inspire and enable people to spread your story in a way that generates a R.O.B. (Return on Belief).

THE DIRTY IMBALANCE

There are too many stories today and not enough mouths to spread them.

This imbalance is what causes marketers to take expensive shortcuts. You're reluctant to tell dirty stories because they might spread. So you tell clean stories which are almost guaranteed not to spread.

Your words and actions must be special. You must give people a reason to talk about you in a way you deem favorable to achieving your objectives. There are only two reasons people talk about a marketer's offerings; delight or disdain.

Customers experiencing disdain for your offering are much more likely to talk about you. Conversely, customers who are delighted with your offering might talk about you if they're inspired and it's easy to do so.

That's what this section is about.

The imbalance between stories and mouths that exists today requires your words and deeds to be more than special. If they are indeed special, they must also come equipped with the tools necessary so people may spread them with passion and ease.

Identifying worldviews, revealing imperfection, and co-creating story are important but not enough if your objective is to spread your story via word of mouth.

If you want your story to spread you must outfit it with a will and a way.

The will is inspiration.

The way is to empower.

EMBEDDING DIRT

Embeds are not impartial.

It's why the Department of Defense embedded journalists with the service members who first invaded Iraq. Even with embedded journalists, the government understood it would not be able to definitively control the story. However, embeds did allow it to steer the story in a favorable direction.

Journalists who chose to embed themselves with the military traded a piece of their impartiality for front line access. While they received access they otherwise would not have, they also ceded a bit of their objectivity in that they were forced to rely on the very people they were reporting on for their safety.

Embedding creates advantages.

For storytellers, embedding dirt inspires and enables story to spread.

Consider for a moment why traditionally dirty stories spread. Not the kind I'm advocating you tell. I'm talking about salacious, profane, or obscene stories. Traditionally dirty stories are embedded with both the inspiration and means required to spread wide and far. They are often:

- Indecent
- Funny
- Counterintuitive
- Polarizing
- Offensive
- Pandering

- Reflective of an unexpressed or under expressed worldview
- Inspiring to share
- Easy to share

When you embed a will and a way you are giving others what they need to spread your story.

DIRTY STORIES GO VIRAL

A 28-year old woman who says a former school teacher sexually abused her 16 years earlier told a story that went viral in January 2014.

The woman, who says the abuse started when she was 12, says when she finally found the courage to report her former teacher to authorities she learned the statute of limitations had expired.

With no other option the woman says she felt compelled to contact her former teacher, confront her about the abuse, and finally demand answers to the questions she had been asking herself for so long. During the call, a woman who is identified as the teacher accused of abuse suggests she regrets what happened, is ashamed, and disgusted by her behavior.

The alleged victim had recorded the entire conversation. Shortly after posting a video of the call online, the woman sent a link to the video to her former teacher. The teacher immediately resigned her position as a school administrator and the video quickly went viral with more than 1.4 million views.

Dirty Storytelling

The story contains all of the elements necessary to be compelling:

- **Revelation-** Child was abused
- **Inciting Incident-** The abuser was never brought to justice
- **Quest to restore balance-** Woman finally decides to report abuse
- **Conflict-** Statute of limitations has expired
- **Reaction-** Woman decides to confront teacher
- **Climax-** Teacher admits abuse during confrontation
- **Resolution-** Woman protects other students by prompting teacher to resign

But the story also contains obvious triggers that inspired and empowered others to share it. Without these triggers the story would still qualify as compelling. However, it may not have spread as it did.

Great stories don't spread by themselves.

They spread because someone purposefully designs them to do so.

MUDSLIDES IGNITE GROWTH

Mother Nature's mudslides are destructive.

The kind we're trying to trigger are constructive.

If you believe the majority of messages are irrelevant to the masses then by default you likely believe we are largely back to word of mouth to spread messages that matter.

Triggering word of mouth mudslides is how you grow today.

Sling all the mud you want. But unless that mud is aimed at people who care about it, the mud is likely to miss its mark. But getting your mud in the right hands is not enough. More is required of modern storytellers.

Purposefully designing stories to spread requires attention from the outset. It's difficult to embed triggers after you've finished building a story. The issue of spreadability is not one that can always be fixed in post production.

You can't just throw up a social bar on your site and expect results.

Instead, design your story with purpose.

Embed the tools needed to spread it.

Plan for the word of mouth mudslide you want to create.

THE FILTHY CHANGE

Ever been heralded, recognized, or earned a raise for maintaining the status quo?

Protecting tradition is noble only when tradition is worthy and timeless.

Otherwise, mistaking outdated convention for strategic heirlooms deserving of generational passage is not a viable long term plan.

Be selfish for just a moment here. What do you get by investing in dirty storytelling? Until now, the focus of the book has been on the prospect or customer. But what is it that we want from them? What do we hope to accomplish by telling dirty stories?

Filthy change is what we want.

We spend time changing how they feel so they'll change what they do. We want them to provide an email address, share our story, or buy our product.

The ultimate goal is change.

Clean stories don't change anyone. They don't surprise, arouse emotion, or otherwise prompt people to feel anything. Unless you're willing to get dirty in your storytelling you cannot expect people to feel differently than they already do. People who are not convinced to feel differently about something have no reason to change their behavior.

It's why changing how they feel is so crucial.

Bringing about that change is what sets the table for a word of mouth mudslide. While it's possible to evoke this type of dramatic change in one shot, it often takes stubborn persistence.

A slow but steady drip of dirty stories is often required to bring about the necessary change. It means a single blog post, newsletter, or marketing brochure may simply be components of a larger dirty storytelling strategy. However, each smaller tactic still carries with it the potential to change someone.

But you have to ask properly.

Clean storytellers are often guilty of improperly asking for what they want. Their calls to action often lack courage just like their stories. Clean stories are often generic and free of risk. So too are their calls to action.

Why not take risks with your CTAs?

Dirty storytellers will learn to take risks in their CTAs just as they do in their narratives. Their CTAs may be obnoxiously overt or smoothly subtle. Custom CTAs may be created for specific pieces of content. Different CTAs will be tested socially and in your email marketing. The CTA that produces greater change will guide you in producing future CTAs.

If you spend the time telling a unique story doesn't it make sense to ask for what you want in a unique way? The CTA is no time to get shy. Dirty storytellers are the brave souls who have made revelations of imperfection. Be bold in your CTAs as well.

Unique and specific CTAs bring about change.

But they're not the only triggers for word of mouth mudslides.

DIRTY MEASUREMENT

When you work this hard to tell a story people believe and spread you deserve to know whether your efforts are paying off.

If you're in the business of changing people you'll have to measure for that change. But I'm urging you to measure your dirty marketing efforts differently.

Yes, please benchmark your clean storytelling efforts but not traditionally. Dirty storytellers are not concerned with impressions, eyeballs, or audience sizes.

Dirty storytellers are only concerned about change.

Dirty Storytelling

In addition to your overall marketing objectives, consider allowing your unique and specific CTAs to dictate what you measure. Remember, you can A/B split test your CTAs on Facebook, Twitter, or with your email list for quick measurements.

Otherwise, dirty storytellers might consider allowing CPDE, or cost per dirty engagement, to guide their measurement efforts. The key to success here is specifically defining engagement.

Engagement must ultimately include the change you desire. Only by identifying what prompts conversions will you then be in a position to scale that action. When you scale a high conversion action your sales metrics will ultimately tell you whether you are measuring what matters.

But let's back up for the skeptical.

If you're a clean storyteller and have been resistant thus far to getting dirty I'm hoping you'll consider taking a few measurements. I'd like for you to run a series of A/B split tests and compare clean and dirty stories side by side.

Reduce your anxiety and risk by using small sample sets. For instance, use just a sliver of your email list. Or run side by side advertisements to select Facebook audiences. Be both discreet and daring.

Tell both a clean story and a dirty story and compare the results:

- Which is shared more frequently?
- Which drives more site traffic?

- Which results in greater time spent per page?
- Which results in more subscriber conversions?

If you're so risk averse you're not willing to run these tests on small sample sets but still curious about how clean compares with dirty, hire focus groups. The limitations I discussed earlier in regard to focus groups do not apply here. You're not probing for hidden customer insight or product development guidance. You're only using focus groups to measure and compare.

Tell a clean story to one and a dirty story to the other. Ask a series of questions immediately after the stories are told:

- What do you remember?
- Why do you think you remember that?
- Do you feel differently after hearing the story?
- If not, why?
- If so, what might that feeling cause you to do?
- If the story is one you'd tell to others, why?

A week later check back with your focus groups and see what they recall. Ask a similar set of questions and identify whether time impacted what they recall, how they feel, and whether they did or still plan to do what they said they might.

Now compare the recall data you have for the clean and dirty stories.

If your results are consistent with the tests I've run on:

- Blog post titles
- Email subject lines
- Social post titles
- Advertisement recall

Dirty stories consistently outperform clean stories when measured by recall, believability, engagement, and willingness to share.

Remember, you don't have to be dirty every time.

The credibility your dirt earns will positively impact your cleaner content.

RETURN ON BELIEF

The believable that spreads due only to shock value is not likely to generate a long term return. The unbelievable that doesn't spread is guaranteed not to generate any return at all.

Unless you're concerned only with ego, search engine optimization, or misguided measurement strategies you're likely not content with blending in.

Your only choice then, if you're interested in spreading your idea, is to be believable. Dirty stories are the type that generate a R.O.B.; a return on belief.

Clean stories do not often generate a return. There is nothing remarkable about them. Nothing in clean stories inspires others to pass them on to those they influence.

Each clean story you tell is a cost.

In addition to generating no return, the time spent creating clean stories is costly as well. Clean stories are a tax on your resources and consume effort that could be better utilized elsewhere.

If you're in business to make a difference, demand a return from the stories you tell. It's up to you how you define that return. However, only those willing to risk something in story can expect a return.

Make something in which people can believe.

Then generate a return by providing the triggers people need to spread the belief.

25 TRIGGERS TO SPREAD YOUR STORY

Embed these triggers in the stories you tell to inspire and enable others to tell those they influence.

1. WARNING LABELS

Include a label on your offering that warns people of the potential consequences associated with using the offering. Research indicates warning labels can actually build trust with consumers. Companies that include labels, especially when they're not required to do so, are often perceived as more honest than those that do not. Organizations that attach labels that warn of negative consequences may be perceived as genuinely caring for their customers despite the risk their offering poses. If labels might resonate with your audience, consider warning it of a lesser known or overlooked consequence. Labels that warn of potentially negative consequences may be advantageous to you as human nature often desires the forbidden. Labels may also be used counterintuitively to warn people about the outsized benefits of using your product. **WARNING:** Implementing the ideas in this book may ignite uncontrollable growth resulting in increased market share, reduced marketing costs, and longer vacations for you!

2. LEVERAGE HATERS

Rather than first distributing a story to those with whom you believe it'll resonate, consider first telling the story to those you know will hate it. This works well for particularly polarizing brands. Polarization can be an advantage if used wisely. Engage groups of consumers that you know passionately dislike your offering. Annoy, agitate, and poke people who'll never buy your offering but are likely to talk publicly about how abhorrent it is. Why? Poking your adversaries will rally your base of dedicated supporters. When your loyal customers see you being attacked, they are likely to come to your defense publicly and amplify the conversation. If your brand lacks polarization you can work to create it by flipping your marketing efforts. Identify your most imperfect customer, clarify why your offering is not for them, and agitate them publicly. **WARNING:** Manufacturing polarization may negatively impact your reputation. Proceed with caution.

3. ORCHESTRATE A BAN

Causing your offering to be banned in some way will stimulate demand for it. Major League Baseball receives more correspondence in support of Pete Rose and Joe Jackson than any of its other tens of thousands of players. Rose was banned from baseball for life as was Jackson. Fans worldwide write letters, sign petitions, and lead grassroots campaigns demanding the two be reinstated so they're eligible for the Hall of Fame. Similarly, organizations that create commercials that are banned or do not meet network requirements for broadcast are often viewed more than if they had actually been broadcast. Bans create intrigue, demand, and buzz. Should you decide to ban this book from your office please tell the world!

4. PROMPT CEASE & DESIST ORDERS

Organizations sincerely trying to make a difference, innovate, or otherwise disrupt an existing business may actually benefit from receiving cease and desist orders. A cease and desist order, so long as the organization in receipt of the order is sincere in its business intentions, should post the order online for all to see. Why? It's likely to generate sympathy from those who may benefit from the organization's invention. A cease and desist order may indicate the organization is being targeted by a patent troll or a market leader attempting to crush an upstart. Those who may benefit from disruption are likely to spread the story in a way they otherwise would not had a cease and desist order never been sent.

5. TOUCH THE TABOO

Taboos are opportunities to challenge convention, reframe an issue, or buck the status quo. Offerings that empower people to do something they are currently forbidden from doing due to a cultural taboo embed their marketing in the offering. If not, identify taboos you can connect your offering with in some way. Identify something currently forbidden or culturally unacceptable you can reinforce, challenge, or at which you may poke fun. Taboos are opportunities to violate expectations. Cultural norms are routinely being redefined. What was forbidden or not spoken of publicly a generation ago may be commonplace today. Use these shifts in values to spread your story.

6. ENGINEER SCARCITY

One of the first questions an investor will ask is whether your idea is scalable. Ideas that aren't scalable are often seen as less attractive to profit-hungry investors. However, engineering scarcity around your marketing efforts can create more demand than scaling might. When you limit, delete, or make something unavailable at a certain point in the future you create more demand for it in the short term. Legitimate scarcity will trigger buzz and demand from those who do not want to miss out on that which is scarce. **WARNING:** Feigning scarcity is transparently selfish and has the potential to create a backlash that results in an erosion of loyalty.

7. GO LIVE

Telling your story in front of a live audience is helpful in spreading your idea quickly. Live is risky and often challenging to deliver without complication. That's why it commands attention and causes people to care. Look for opportunities to tell your story live. Involve vendors, customers, or other stakeholders. Live events are opportunities that position you at the front of the room rather than the back.

8. DRAMATIZE THE MUNDANE

This is a counterintuitive technique designed to attract attention and stimulate imagination. Dramatizing the mundane allows you to reframe an issue. The technique works best when paired with metaphor, humor, or personification. Your offering may be a boring household product. But when you use a metaphor to dramatize your offering you create the potential for prospects to see it differently than they had previously.

9. MINIMIZE THE VOLATILE

This too is a counterintuitive technique that causes an audience to take a second look and consider minor perceptional adjustments. Minimizing the volatile may be effectively paired with humor or metaphor and used to persuade incrementally. In other words, it won't be believable if you attempt to drastically minimize the power of a volcano, the ferocity of a shark, or the fear caused by a tsunami. However, the technique may help people make minor adjustments to their perceptions that cause them to consider your call to action in a way they may not have in the past.

10. CREATE A CHORUS

Rock stars don't have to sing the choruses in their songs. They can simply point the microphone toward the crowd and their fans will sing the chorus verbatim. An opportunity exists in story to train your audience to do the same. It may take the form of a popular brand tag line, quirky slogan, or humorous question. Whatever form it takes it should be short, memorable, and indicative of your brand. You must also be able to evoke your chorus with a cue. This is key in using the technique as a trigger. Condition an audience to sing you the chorus after receiving the cue.

11. SHOW INSTEAD OF TELL

What might you show an audience that speaks louder than words? The idea is to provide your audience with something it can then show others. The absence of words, a marketing brochure, or an official announcement will steer attention toward what you are revealing. What type of picture, piece of video, or rendering might you "leak" to your audience? Consider taking a page from Apple and "accidentally" leaving behind a drawing of a next generation iPhone at a bar. Besides triggering story you may also use this technique to do market research.

12. WHAT KIND OF LOSER ARE YOU?

How you lose can trigger others to spread your story. Sore losers certainly get a lot of attention but trigger stories that aren't always favorable to their reputations. Conversely, a loser who uses the experience for good creates an opportunity to, at times, earn more attention, trust, and loyalty than the winner of the contest. How? When you lose a customer, a contract, or contest consider identifying exactly why and help others avoid such a fate. Teach, tell, and train others to avoid the mistakes you have made. Pass on the lessons you learned. Show others how to help those they serve. Your generosity will not go unnoticed.

13. RATTLE A HORNET'S NEST

Position yourself as a leader by picking fights with those above you that are deserving of them. Publicly call out unsafe work environments, unsavory business practices, or tactics used to manipulate victims. Only fight up and only fight those who are wrong. Be prepared for blowback and to offer solutions. Don't be transparently selfish and tout yourself as the industry model. People will discover this for themselves as long as your intentions are noble, honest, and just.

14. KILLER FIRST & LAST LINES

The first line of your speech, presentation, or corporate video is the most valuable real estate you have in terms of storytelling. Don't waste it with small talk, an insincere greeting, or a cliché. Your first line colors the rest of your offering. Make it memorable by surprising people with it. It makes little difference how it surprises so long as it communicates to your audience that it had better pay attention because this is not a run of the mill story. The last line is the second most important piece of real estate in story. Wrap your story with a memorable last line that calls your audience to action overtly or covertly. You'll get extra credit if your first and last lines are the same, but have dual meanings.

15. CREATE A NONVERBAL CHORUS

Similar to creating a verbal cue that elicits a chorus-like response from an audience you may also accomplish the same with a gesture. Consider how a gesture, movement, or nonverbal form of communication may elicit a desired response. Both verbal and nonverbal responses prompt an audience to participate and share the story. Professional wrestlers are actually better at this than many professional communicators. Wrestlers train their audiences to automatically respond to cues. An audience that understands when and how to respond to your nonverbal cues will finish your sentences and tell others about you.

16. EMBED GENEROSITY

In a world of takers a giver will stand out. Approach your product design, web site layout, or customer service from the perspective of a prospect. Identify ways to be generous each step of the way. Give special consideration to being generous after a sale. While generosity can take the form of a coupon, discount, or bonus it may also be intangible. No matter what form it takes, as long as it is sincere, generosity can trigger a word of mouth mudslide.

17. FLIP YOUR CTA

Calls to action generally promise value in return for action. Understand though people are often much more motivated by the fear of losing something than they are by the optimism of gaining something. Many calls to action frame what the prospect stands to gain by subscribing. Consider flipping your CTA to highlight what a consumer will lose or miss out on by not signing up. Run split tests to see if flipping your CTA results in more conversions.

18. SIGNAGE THAT BEGS A QUESTION

Signage that creates ambiguity stimulates the imagination. Resist the urge to answer every question your customer may have. Provide an opportunity for them to wonder what you actually mean. Be mindful not take this too far. It won't work for producers of commodities or with customers seeking consistency or precisely measured products. However, you can start small. Beg a question by giving a range for your discount, erasing what customers have come to expect, or creating a possibility that reaches to infinity.

19. TEST YOURSELF THE WAY A CHILD MIGHT

Identify how your product or service is or could be used off-label. This trigger combines elements of the "taboo" and "show instead of tell" triggers. How might a child who hasn't read the directions first interact with your product? When you incorporate off-label or alternative uses into your marketing you're communicating that you know your customers intimately. You are applauding them for their creativity. You may also use humor to curb an off-label use that could harm a customer. Either way, putting a less rigid side of your organization on display can trigger your story to spread.

20. PERSONIFY YOUR OFFERING

Represent your offering, idea, or organization as a human being. This works especially well for boring, complex, or commoditized offerings. Assigning human qualities to inanimate objects can soften them, make them real, and cause them to become more memorable. Use this technique to humanize your offering by aligning with stereotypical personas your audience likes, trusts, and respects.

21. HELP SOMEONE BUT DON'T TELL ANYONE

Identify disasters, accidents, or unexpected challenges your offering is well-suited to mitigate. Preposition resources, offer them in advance, or show up after the fact without issuing a news release. Do this because you want to and because it's something your customers would be proud to support. Do not do this if your intent is to market yourself as a hero. I hesitated to include this in the trigger section as I find insincere cause marketing particularly disturbing. However, I included it as I am convinced business can save lives our governments do not. Remember, our federal government made it to Baghdad for war quicker than Baton Rouge after Hurricane Katrina. Right or wrong, when you act on that which is in your heart it will be revealed.

22. OFFEND THE UNWORTHY

The award you choose not to accept, the dinner you opt not to attend, or the gala you conveniently skip says as much or more about you than your marketing. This trigger is similar to picking a fight with those deserving of one. Think hard about why you might be receiving an invitation. Probe deeply as to whether you'd be receiving the invitation if the circumstances were different. Just because it's "for a good cause" doesn't mean it's a worthy, noble, or deserving cause. Don't allow the invitation to flatter your ego and blind you to reality.

23. ANNOY THE WORLD

This technique works well for commodities. If the customers you serve make purchasing decisions based solely or largely on price, annoy them. Create insidious jingles, ludicrous brand tag lines, or hire an obnoxious spokesperson or animal. The more annoying or polarizing, the better. The key is to be annoyingly memorable but not offensive.

24. HIDE, BARTER, & BAIL

Provide unexpected customer service by hiding something in your offering because you get a kick out of delighting customers, not solely to trigger the spread of story. Hide a handwritten thank you note, tickets to a ball game, or a one hundred dollar bill in your offering. Separately, break into new markets or attract a different type of customer by offering to trade products or services. You might even partner with your neighbors and organize a *"Bartering on the Block"* event to entice prospects to try your entry level offering. Separately, you might also consider bailing or closing your business for a day to support a worthy cause or to reward your employees. Offer customers incentives to spread the word about how shopping the day before you bail will benefit a worthy cause or deserving employee.

25. DELIGHT SPONTANEOUSLY

You can't always embed triggers. Instead of looking only for ways to spread your story look for ways to delight someone in real time. Actively look for opportunities to surprise, exceed expectations, and over deliver. The harder you look the more of these opportunities you're likely to find. When this becomes second nature you won't need to embed triggers or spend money on marketing. Your story will spread organically because you'll become the story. The one that spontaneously delights.

Visit **dirtystorytelling.com** for updated triggers, fresh ideas, and additional tools designed to help your story spread.

STORY TRIGGER WORKSHEET

Answering the questions or completing the scenarios on this worksheet will help you create a list of ideas you can use to build personalized triggers that inspire and enable others to spread your story.

I. WARNING LABELS

1. If you were the customer what might the organization voluntarily warn you about that would cause you to trust the organization more?

2. Are there off-label use concerns or lesser known risks you could warn customers about?

3. What benefits or positive outcomes might you humorously warn customers of?

II. LEVERAGE HATERS

1. Who passionately dislikes your offering and how likely are they to vocalize their feelings?

2. If the groups identified are vocal, what could you do to politely bother them?

III. ORCHESTRATE A BAN

1. In what ways or from where might your product or service lend itself to being banned?

2. What type of customer insight might help you forecast a possible increase in demand should your offering be banned from a store, conference, or online community? Might you test your hypothesis on a crowdfunding site?

IV. PROMPT CEASE & DESIST ORDERS

1. Would a cease and desist order result in lost business? If so, how much?

2. If not or if you deem the loss a strategic investment, how might you prompt a cease and desist letter from a patent troll or market leader?

V. TOUCH THE TABOO

1. What is forbidden or culturally unacceptable to discuss in your industry? What would happen if you addressed these issues as an antagonist or humorously?

VI. ENGINEER SCARCITY

1. Which pieces of the story you want to tell are in short supply?

2. How might you alert prospects or customers to this shortage?

VII. GO LIVE

1. Which pieces of your story could be performed live?

2. Which pieces of the narrative currently produced behind the scenes could be performed in a more engaging fashion if done live?

VIII. DRAMATIZE THE MUNDANE

1. What's boring about your offering or industry?

2. For each item listed above, note the opposite.

3. Identify metaphors for the items listed after question 2 that you can use to represent and dramatize the items listed after question 1.

IX. MINIMIZE THE VOLATILE

1. What do people avoid, dislike, or hate about your offering or industry?

2. In what ways might it be appropriate and effective to use humor or metaphor to prompt minor adjustments to these perceptions?

X. CREATE A CHORUS

1. What feelings do your brand tag line inspire?

2. How might you frame those feelings as cues designed to prompt an audience to voluntarily repeat or say your tag line?

XI. SHOW INSTEAD OF TELL

1. What kinds of "confidential" pictures, videos, or renderings might you "leak" to trigger story?

2. What must you leak so you can use the response to improve the product or service under development?

XII. WHAT KIND OF LOSER ARE YOU?

1. What mistakes did you identify or lessons did you learn the last time you lost a customer, client, or contract?

2. How might you creatively teach others to perform better than you did?

XIII. RATTLE A HORNET'S NEST

1. List the unsafe practices, manipulative tactics, or inefficiencies evident in your industry?

2. How might you creatively and publicly acknowledge these issues and solve them for the entire industry?

XIV. KILLER FIRST & LAST LINES

1. If your audience saw how your offering was created what might surprise them?

2. Turn those surprises into first lines that create intrigue.

XV. CREATE A NONVERBAL CHORUS

1. In what ways do you want your audience to respond to your story?

2. What types of nonverbal cues might you link with the desired responses and how will you condition your audience to connect them?

XVI. EMBED GENEROSITY

1. Which parts of the sales process do customers in your industry try to avoid, perceive as greedy, or consider high pressure?

XVII. FLIP YOUR CTA

1. What will your audience lose or miss out on should it choose not to join your email list?

2. Frame this loss in your CTA as something that may be avoided by joining.

XVIII. SIGNAGE THAT BEGS A QUESTION

1. List the standard, cliché, or expected signs that adorn businesses in your industry?

2. How might you delete, stretch, or rearrange components of these signs in ways that cause people to notice, wonder, or fill in the blanks?

XIX. TEST YOURSELF THE WAY A CHILD MIGHT

1. How is or how might your product be used off-label or by a child for the first time?

2. How might you position this unintended use, amplify its benefit, or humorously discourage potentially harmful uses?

XX. PERSONIFY YOUR OFFERING

1. If your product, service, or organization were a person, who would it be?

2. What story would that person tell about your offering?

XXI. HELP SOMEONE BUT DON'T TELL ANYONE

1. What disaster or emergency might your offering help mitigate quickly?

2. What's keeping you from committing to help in the event of a disaster?

XXII. OFFEND THE UNWORTHY

1. List the events or "good causes" to which you are routinely invited or regularly participate.

2. Why are these good causes? How do you know? When is the last time you studied the disclosures these groups are required to make?

XXIII. ANNOY THE WORLD

1. What is boring, mundane, or unremarkable about the offering you sell?

2. What is contradictory to the boring, mundane, or unremarkable traits listed above? How might you make these opposing traits obnoxious in ways that are annoyingly memorable yet not offensive?

XXIV. HIDE, BARTER, & BAIL

1. What could you hide in your offering that would thank a customer in a way words cannot?

2. What could you offer as a trade that might lead to a new customer?

3. Who could you help if you were to bail or close for a day and what incentives would you offer customers to help?

XXV. DELIGHT SPONTANEOUSLY

1. List the most ridiculous or outlandish ways you might exceed a customer's expectations, list roughly what that would cost, and why you can't afford to do it.

2. Identify your most valuable customer and what he or she will spend with you over the lifetime of the relationship.

3. Think again about your answers to question one.

Nick Winkler

THE DIRTY STORYTELLING HALL OF FAME

The elite dirty storytellers are valuable to those who matter, in part, because of the selfless revelations they courageously make for the benefit of others.

THE DIRTY STORYTELLING HALL OF FAME

Before I reveal 101 real world dirty storytelling examples, it's important you understand the company you'll be in when you begin telling dirty stories.

Dirty storytellers come in a variety of shapes, sizes, and statures. This is one reason why dirty stories are so special. Dirty storytelling provides anyone with guts the means to inject authenticity and believability into marketing.

Dirty stories do not discriminate.

You can be rich, poor, or in between and still tell dirty stories. Dirty stories are friends of the truth wherever it lies and with whoever speaks it. You need nothing other than courage to tell dirty stories.

Should dirty storytelling become pervasive the dishonest will be exposed simply because they are tellers of clean stories. Only those who use deception, manipulation, and spin must fear the spread of dirty stories. It's why it is right to briefly spotlight some of the most elite dirty storytellers of all time.

The *Dirty Storytelling Hall of Fame* is reserved for those willing to take risks for the benefit of others. The *Hall* is reserved only for those who put their own skin in the game before asking others to commit. I hope you'll strive to market like those in the *Dirty Storytelling Hall of Fame.*

They are the dirtiest of the dirty.

JESUS CHRIST

Jesus is the King of dirty storytellers.

Imagine yourself in a business situation similar to The Last Supper. Could you look at a small but adoring group of customers and predict that soon they would betray you and shift their business to a competitor?

Knowing this betrayal would ultimately lead to the death of your business, would you then pamper and feed the one you know will betray you?

The prediction of betrayal Jesus makes is the ultimate dirty revelation. Not only does Jesus embrace the conflict at hand, He knows how it will turn out and commands Judas to get on with what he is going to do.

I'm certainly not picking a fight with biblical scholars over whether Jesus allowed the betrayal so it would allow for the fulfillment of God's plan or whether Jesus was destined to be crucified regardless of Judas' betrayal. I'm simply illuminating how the betrayal of Jesus contains all of the elements necessary for a dirty story.

Jesus was right about Judas and Peter.

But it's the last commandment Jesus gives his disciples following Judas' departure that business leaders might benefit from most. Jesus, in his *Farewell Discourse*, tells them to love one another like He has loved them.

It is Jesus' final wish.

Imagine if we treated prospects, customers, and former customers in such a way.

He is risen indeed! Hallelujah!

174

DOMINO'S PIZZA

Domino's is the dirtiest pizza maker in the game.
Slinging mud is exactly why the pizza chain is taking
market share in an otherwise growth stagnant category.
The chain is outperforming its competition in nearly
every metric that matters thanks, in part, to the dirty
stories it tells.

After reinventing itself and igniting growth with a
dirty documentary that acknowledged its pizza tasted
like cardboard in 2009, the pizza king is back for a dirty
encore in 2014. Domino's has created a video it calls,
"Failure is an option." The commercial features
Domino's executives acknowledging not everything the
pizza maker tries is going to work.

To get better, the pizza chain tells its customers it's
going to fall short along the way.

Domino's then pokes fun at an offering that recently
crashed and burned. An executive asks, "Ever heard of
our cookie pizza?" The video then cuts to a Domino's
chef uncomfortably holding a cookie pizza box and
muttering, "I don't wanna talk about it." Her remark is
followed by an awkward moment of silence before
employees explain how not giving up after mistakes is
what allows them to create menu items that become
much more popular than the cookie pizza.

The commercial ends with Scott Hinshaw, Domino's
Executive Vice President of Operations, saying
confidently, "We cannot be afraid to fail. It sounds
crazy but it's who we are."

CHAEL SONNEN

Chael Sonnen is a mixed martial artist who fought professionally in the UFC and a self-proclaimed "bad guy".

On the contrary, he's dirty good.

Sonnen is not a *Dirty Hall of Famer* because of his professional wrestling like post-fight interviews. He's not one of the dirtiest because of his prowess in front of a camera or on a microphone. Sonnen is one of the dirtiest because he is authentic.

The low hanging fruit has been well-documented. What's important regarding Sonnen, considered the best promoter of fights in mixed martial arts, is that he believes insincerely hyping a fight is fraudulent. Sonnen believes fans who pay to see a fight deserve refunds when the fighters involved manufacture conflict.

Sonnen says, "I feel if you are trying to get somebody to, to purchase something from you, even if it's a fight, and you misrepresented why it is you're fighting or what the conflict is, I just find that's dishonest."

But this isn't why Sonnen is a *Hall of Famer* either.

In his book *The Voice of Reason*, Sonnen reveals the insecurities, loneliness, and shyness that plague many of the world's toughest professional fighters. He knocks down the façade fighters construct and allows readers a glimpse behind the curtain.

He also outlines the mistakes he made that cost him careers in real estate and politics. He recounts exactly how he lost a world championship fight by allowing his mind to wander to the promise he made his father, on his father's death bed, that one day he'd become a world champion.

Even dirtier, Sonnen recalls an intimate and surprising moment between he and his father moments after learning his father is dying of cancer. It's too beautifully dirty to spoil here. However, it alone is worth the price of the book.

You may not fight other people but you're fighting something. It means you'll benefit from studying Sonnen's stories.

Tough guys aren't supposed to cry. Nor are they to admit they're afraid. Sonnen does both publicly.

The bad guy isn't really bad.

He's just admirably dirty.

SONGWRITERS

The songwriters included in the *Hall* are antitheses of the condescending blasphemous hacks Steven Pressfield describes in *The War of Art*. In other words, these songwriters don't sit down to write hit songs.

They write songs that must be written.

Rather than attempt to capture the dirt in song with words, I've simply included a song or three next to each songwriter. The songwriters may or may not have written each of the songs beside their names. But each is reflective of what they write.

If you want to tell dirty stories study their work.

- **Guy Clark**- "The Guitar", "Black Haired Boy", "The Cape"
- **Robert Earl Keen**- "Think It Over One Time", "Lynville Train", "I Would Change My Life"
- **John Prine**- "Souvenirs", "Some Humans Ain't Human", "Hello in There"
- **Chris Knight**- "A Train Not Running", "Blame Me", "Enough Rope"
- **Joe Ely**- "Letters to Laredo", "Gallo del Cielo"
- **Jason Boland**- "Sons and Daughters of Dixie", "Farmer's Luck", "Dark and Dirty Mile"

PAUL GRAHAM

Paul Graham is dirty generous.

Graham is a venture capitalist best known for co-founding the *Y Combinator*, a firm which provides seed money to hundreds of startup companies like Airbnb, Dropbox, and Stripe. But the dreams he helps turn into realities are not why he's on this list.

Graham is a *Dirty Hall of Famer* because of the collection of essays he has been posting online at **paulgraham.com** since 2001. Graham's essays, which I am severely oversimplifying, detail how to think or generate ideas, how to raise money or avoid being distracted by it, and how to avoid mistakes and leverage failure to succeed.

Rarely is the world treated to an insider's perspective as detailed, actionable, and valuable as Graham's. Graham shows his hand in ways other venture capitalists do not. His generosity is unique and a gift even to those who are not technically savvy.

In an essay titled, *What We Look for in Founders*, Graham details the qualities he looks for when investing in founders of companies. Determination tops the list but it's the fourth quality, naughtiness, in which Graham outlines the benefit of the dirty intangible. Graham describes the virtue of naughtiness like this;

"Though the most successful founders are usually good people, they tend to have a piratical gleam in their eye. They're not Goody Two-Shoes type good. Morally, they care about getting the big questions right, but not about observing proprieties. That's why I'd use the word naughty rather than evil. They delight in breaking rules, but not rules that matter. This quality may be redundant though; it may be implied by imagination.

Sam Altman of Loopt is one of the most successful alumni, so we asked him what question we could put on the Y Combinator application that would help us to discover more people like him. He said to ask about a time when they'd hacked something to their advantage—hacked in the sense of beating the system, not breaking into computers. It has become one of the questions we pay most attention to when judging applications."

The mud Graham routinely slings is the advantage of which Altman speaks.

Dirty Storytelling

Very seldom is the world treated to the answers prior to the test.

Graham is a cheat sheet for life.

GARRISON KEILLOR

Garrison Keillor is the dirtiest storyteller on the radio.

Four million people listen to the public radio program he hosts every Saturday night, *A Prairie Home Companion*, which celebrated its 40th anniversary in 2014 in an era where some predicted the internet would make traditional radio irrelevant.

Keillor's unique brand of humor is an acquired taste.

Unless you're born with it.

Keillor observes human behavior, and its comedic value, so perceptively it often strikes some as anything but funny. In a parody of Keillor on the cartoon *The Simpsons*, Homer is perplexed as to why the studio audience is laughing at a Keillor-like monologue and asks, "What the hell's so funny?"

Keillor isn't for everyone.

It's why he's so important to some.

Keillor routinely pokes fun at college English majors, Midwesterners, and their oddities. His monologue, *The News from Lake Wobegon*, starts the same every week, "Well it's been a quiet week in Lake Wobegon, my hometown. Where all the women are strong, all the men are good looking, and all the children are above average."

He sees what we don't.

That is until he reveals it, and its humor, to us.

Nick Winkler

STEVEN PRESSFIELD

I never consciously understood why I wear work boots when I write.

But Steven Pressfield, who wears work boots when he writes as well, helped me understand what's going on beneath the surface.

Pressfield says creating art is war.

And you don't wear sandals when going to war.

It's a war against self-sabotage that is fueled by a crippling fear Pressfield says is the most toxic force on the planet and the root of unhappiness—*The Resistance*.

His book, *The War of Art*, identifies and names this enemy which works within us all and attempts to prevent us from achieving the life God intended for us. Not only does Pressfield identify the enemy and how it manifests itself, he also prescribes measures to overcome Resistance.

Pressfield exposes Resistance for what it is: an evil killer of achievement.

After reading *The War of Art* it seemed silly to me to ever write another book. The world has what it needs in Pressfield's masterpiece—the dirtiest book ever written. Please read it and give it to those you love.

Pressfield shows us all how to win the war.

He is peerless.

The best we can do is lace up our work boots and follow his lead.

101 DIRTY STORYTELLING EXAMPLES

1. Marketer Britten Follett's customer survey that asked, "How likely would you be to throw this piece of marketing in the trash after receiving it?" which prompted an outpouring of customer goodwill and engagement because of the question's honesty.

2. Former *NBC Nightly News* anchor Tom Brokaw's assessment of the industry he once sat atop, "Now the political news comes at us 24/7 on cable, through the air, the digital universe, on radio and print. And it comes to us more and more as opinion rather than a recitation of the facts as best they can be determined. News is a hit-and-run game, for the most part, with too little accountability for error."

3. Fred Rogers, host of *Mr. Rogers' Neighborhood*, revealing what attracted him to television, "I went into television because I hated it so, and I thought there's some way of using this fabulous instrument to nurture those who would watch and listen."

4. Frank Sinatra's humorous but authentic revelation, "I feel sorry for people that don't drink, because when they wake up in the morning, that is the best they are going to feel all day."

5. The bumper stickers that warn, "This truck insured by Smith & Wesson."

6. David Newman, author of *Do It! Marketing*, detailing his worst ever sales call so readers can avoid the mistakes he made.

7. Seth Godin revealing he was nervous answering questions live from marketing students on a Google hangout chat because future viewers of the video aren't likely to understand the rough spots being live can create.

8. The billboard German razor blade maker Martor uses to show why its blades are the sharpest that includes plastic pigeons, which presumably tried to land on the razor-shaped billboard, cut in half and lying on the ground nearby.

9. The neon safety vests and hard hats the Indiana Department of Transportation erects to symbolize those who have died in construction work zone accidents and uses as reminders to slow down.

10. Warren Buffet's invitation to critics to challenge his investing prowess in front of tens of thousands of fans at his annual meeting in Omaha.

11. *Mad Money* host Jim Cramer's public admissions regarding stock market recommendations that have not been profitable.

12. Country music singer Garth Brooks thanking fans for buying his music despite his admission he can't sing or play the guitar all that well.

13. The late Daniel Patrick Moynihan, sociologist and U.S. Senator, who courageously warned, "...A community that allows a large number of men to grow up in broken families, dominated by women, never acquiring any stable relationship to male authority, never acquiring any set of rational expectations about the future -- that community asks for and gets chaos. Crime, violence, unrest, disorder -- most particularly the furious, unrestrained lashing out at the whole social structure -- that is not only to be expected; it is very near to inevitable. And it is richly deserved."

14. Author Steven Pressfield's kick in the pants on overcoming fear, not selling out, and being authentic in *The War of Art*.

15. Media mogul Rupert Murdoch on disruption, "When you're a catalyst for change, you make enemies- and I'm proud of the ones I've got."

16. Author Robert McKee's reminder that the world is asking that we risk rejection, ridicule, and failure in pursuit of meaning and beauty in his book *Story*.

17. Professional wrestler Ric Flair on his age and how it impacts his performance versus younger athletes, "You know the thing about *Space Mountain*? It's the oldest ride in the park but it's still got the longest line. Woooooooooooooo!"

18. Academic Robert Cialdini's plea that we use his powerful compliance techniques for good rather than manipulative purposes in his book *Influence.*

19. The glass skull spirits maker Crystal Head Vodka created to package its quartz filtered vodka.

20. MMA fighter Chael Sonnen for revealing the heartbreak he felt after not winning the championship he promised his dead father he would.

21. Author David Horsager for repeatedly telling business leaders trust not money is the currency of life in his book *The Trust Edge.*

22. Storytelling coach Doug Stevenson's directive to transform the listener by going deep and telling the truth in *Story Theatre Method.*

23. *Tell to Win* author Peter Guber's vulnerability in revealing to the world his failures and why many have been the result of failing to tell compelling stories.

24. The successful homeless gentleman on Sandy Blvd. in Portland, OR whose sign read, "I will spend some of your money on beer- just being honest!"

25. North Minneapolis Reverend Jerry McAfee who under fire from critics said, "God's heart doesn't change with time. I preach the Bible, not what's popular."

26. Steve Jobs on the importance of what you do when no one is looking, "When you are a

carpenter making a beautiful chest of drawers, you're not going to use a piece of plywood on the back, even though it faces the wall and nobody will see it. You'll know it's there…to sleep well at night…the quality has to be carried all the way through."

27. Legendary talk radio icon Bill Cunningham's revelation regarding his popularity, "I'm not sure if you know this, but half the people hate me!"

28. Amazon founder Jeff Bezos on moral responsibility in business, "The one thing that offends me most is when I walk by a bank and see ads trying to convince people to take out second mortgages on their homes so they can go on vacation. That's approaching evil."

29. Singer songwriter Norah Jones in "Humble Me," "Went out on a limb, gone too far, broke down at the side of the road…I don't want to call you but you're all I have to turn to."

30. Mack Collier, #blogchat founder and author of *Think Like a Rock Star*, who wears his social media heart on his sleeve so organizations big and small may learn to genuinely turn customers into fans.

31. The last question I asked nearly every person I interviewed as an investigative and general assignment television news reporter, "Is there anything I wasn't smart enough to ask you that I should have?"

32. The billboard a neighboring state is using to poach frustrated residents of Illinois that reads, "Tired of Illinoising? Move to Indiana!"

33. Billionaire NBA team owner Mark Cuban cautioning the world in regard to forcing fellow NBA team owner Donald Sterling to sell his team following racist comments attributed to Sterling.

34. Discount carrier Spirit Airlines CEO Ben Baldanza recognizing who fills the role of the hero in the story his company tells, "Our customers are the smartest because they've found a way to save money on airfare."

35. Author Tom Peters' advice to anyone looking for a shortcut, "Get up first. Go to bed last. Work your ass off in between. Get lucky."

36. *A Prairie Home Companion* host Garrison Keillor on the 40th anniversary of his public radio broadcast that draws 4 million listeners a week, "The best you can hope for really is, when you are young, people instill in you an ambition, a standard that you can never achieve. And you spend your life trying to roll the boulder up the hill."

37. Garrison Keillor on *The Keillor Reader* a collection of his writings marking the 40th anniversary of his radio program *A Prairie Home Companion*, "It was painful to put this book together because those old shows were really not any good. And

I've written a lot that I wish I could delete, but it's not possible."

38. Adultswim.com, an adult comedy producer, announcing its decision to once again make its content available online after betting the internet was dead three years earlier, "…we fu$*ed up…pulled all (our) episodes…and told (everyone) to go to hell. This was the LSD talking!"

39. NBA superstar Kevin Durant's tear-filled 2014 MVP acceptance speech in which he detailed his mother's sacrifices and announced, "You're the real MVP."

40. Becky McCray, a resource and friend of small town and rural businesses, who teaches anyone smart enough to listen about the virtues of doing business according to small town rules.

41. Dale Wimbrow's 1934 poem *The Guy in the Glass*.

42. Walter D. Wintle's poem *Thinking*.

43. Tom Peters, purveyor of excellence, on the responsibility we have to market ourselves in the timeless classic *The Brand Called You*.

44. NBA legend Larry Bird, "Leadership is diving for a loose ball, getting the crowd involved, getting other players involved. It's being able to take it as well as dish it out."

45. Hall of Fame pitcher Greg Maddux, "I daydream just like everybody else. I just do it with my body facing the field, so everybody thinks I'm paying attention."

46. Television News photographer Marlon Hall's assessment of the way managers often order their priorities, "They're majoring in minors."

47. The "Get them off your dog," advertisement placed on a shopping mall floor by Frontline flea and tick spray that, when viewed from above, looks as if shoppers are fleas crawling all over a dog.

48. Richard Branson's blimp that read, "BA Can't Get It Up!!" which hovered over the downed Ferris wheel airline competitor British Airways had sponsored and called a news conference to highlight.

49. Johnny Carson's observation that, "If life were fair, Elvis would be alive and all the impersonators would be dead."

50. Hall of Fame NFL running back Walter Payton identifying different levels of achievement, "When you're good at something you'll tell everyone. When you're great at something, they'll tell you."

51. At home soda machine maker Sodastream's Super Bowl commercial, which was banned because it was offensive to halftime show sponsor Pepsi, that prompted millions of views and the hashtag #sorrycokeandpepsi.

52. Lewis Dvorkin's "incentive-based, entrepreneurial journalism" model at the reinvented Forbes, which pays reporters, in part, based on how popular their stories become.

53. The first line of Britten Follett's child abuse prevention speech in which she shows a picture of a two and a half year-old victim of child abuse and inspires her audiences to make the topic a political issue, "I killed this little girl- we all did!"

54. The "This Can't be a Buick" television commercial the car company uses to ridicule and change its boring reputation by spotlighting the humorous reaction grandmothers have to new Buick offerings.

55. The documentary in which Domino's Pizza admits its product tastes, "...like cardboard...and ketchup..." and tests its reinvented pizza on critics.

56. The title of Scott Adams' book, *How to Fail at Almost Everything and Still Win Big*

57. Gini Dietrich's public relations blog and book, *Spin Sucks.*

58. The milk cartons in which Seth Godin packaged *Purple Cow.*

59. The vans Spirit Airlines packs with female dancers to promote flights to Vegas.

60. The first line of Roger Creager's song "Crazy Again," "My boss is a son of a bitch"...and the subsequent admissions that inspire listeners to stand up for what is right rather than popular.

61. Child behavioral therapist Janet Lehman's marketing materials which include her admission, "I'll never forget the day my child told me they hated me!"

62. The flyers a Minnesota church pastor hangs in bars telling drinkers that the wine is free at church on Sundays.

63. Columnist and political analyst George Will's warning about the future, "Some calamities- the 1929 stock market crash, Pearl Harbor, 9/11- have come like summer lightening, as bolts from the blue. The looming crisis of America's Ponzi entitlement structure is different. Driven by the demographics of an aging population, its causes, timing, and scope are known."

64. Robert Earl Keen's song "The Road Goes On and On," which exposes a fellow singer for plagiarizing in ways a lawsuit cannot.

65. The media interviews recovering drug addicts routinely provide at Minnesota Teen & Adult Challenge, which offer others hope that they too can break their addictions.

66. Burrito chain Chipotle's revelation that it cannot source enough meat raised in accordance with what it deems as ethically acceptable practices to accommodate customer demand.

67. The brutally honest but treasured critiques former CBS News correspondent Frank Currier provides to the broadcast news students he mentors and changes.

68. Former Chesapeake Energy CEO Aubrey McClendon on ignorant critics, "I do think a key to success in any walk of life is having a short

memory and a thick skin- I know it has served me well over the years."

69. Any organization that announces it will no longer include fine print after its promotional offers, guarantees, or promises.

70. The tweet Ben & Jerry's created that pokes fun at the hunger often triggered by marijuana and its legalization in Colorado, "BREAKING NEWS: We're hearing reports of stores selling out of Ben & Jerry's in Colorado. What's up with that?"

71. Seven-time world rodeo champion Ty Murray's revelation and advice on riding bulls, "To me the essence of bull riding is so scary and there's so much adrenaline, that if you can stay focused and fluid through that and do your job right, that's a test like no other."

72. Mark Cuban on why entrepreneurs shouldn't always listen to their customers, "Your customers can tell you the things that are broken and how they want to be made happy. Listen to them. Make them happy. But don't rely on them to create the future road map for your product or service. That's your job."

73. Marion Mitchell Morrison, better known by his stage name John Wayne, on entitlement, "I'd like to know why well-educated idiots keep apologizing for lazy and complaining people who think the world owes them a living."

74. Venture capitalist Paul Graham's counterintuitive advice that startups should do

things that don't scale, "The most common unscalable thing founders have to do at the start is to recruit users manually. Nearly all startups have to. You can't wait for users to come to you. You have to go out and get them."

75. The trophies television news reporter Boyd Huppert wins but doesn't tell anyone he gives to the people featured in the stories that actually earn the trophies. Thank you, Sir.

76. The pride of Kaycee, Wyoming and legendary singer Chris LeDoux's revelation, "I can remember sittin' in a café when I first started in rodeo, and waitin' until somebody got done so I could finish what they left."

77. The baseball coach honest enough to say, "You get a lot of people out and deserve it, but you don't throw hard enough to make this team."

78. James Altucher, who advocates bleeding when you blog, and illustrates how we no longer have to wait for someone else to hire, invest in, or pick us in his book, *Choose Yourself.*

79. Comedian Milton Berle on choosing yourself, "If opportunity doesn't knock, build a door."

80. Financial advisor David Armstrong on the benefits of admitting mistakes publicly on his blog, "People like the honesty and maturity that goes with admitting you were wrong."

81. Chuck Norris on the pride that comes from not being a liberal Hollywood actor, "I'm not politically correct in my opinions or my

practice…I will not compromise the truth in any form to cater to others…those who would merely brand me on the Right are oversimplifying and running from the real issue."

82. The two word story online jobs board Careerbuilder.com placed on the roofs of city buses for frustrated high rise office workers to see when looking out their windows, "Don't Jump."

83. Dolly Parton's admission that, "I'm not offended by all the dumb blonde jokes because I know I'm not dumb…and I also know that I'm not blonde."

84. The timing of Amazon CEO Jeff Bezos' December 2013 Christmas shopping rush announcement that the company is experimenting with drones that would deliver packages in 30 minutes within the next five years.

85. Josie LeBalch, a restaurant owner in Santa Monica, who attracted customers without dates on Valentine's Day with her "Bitter Singles Night" promotion.

86. *Meet the Press* moderator Tim Russert dismantling 2004 Colorado Senate candidate Pete Coors, who opposes gay marriage though his beer company sponsors gay festivals, "Why the conflict between the marketing your company does, which in effect tries to pander to the gay community, and these positions which

are opposed to those taken by the gay community?"

87. Activist investor Carl Icahn on being unpopular, "In the takeover business, if you want a friend, you buy a dog."

88. Hedge fund manager Doug Kass on why he temporarily quit Twitter in June 2013, "I've been on twitter for a while now. I try to provide thoughtful tweets that may help traders/investors. But too many haters. As I reflect on Father's Day, life is far too short to be exposed to haters. So I have decided to leave this platform for while."

89. Country music virtuoso Brad Paisley on the feminization of men in his hit song "I'm Still a Guy," "With all of these men linin' up to get neutered, it's hip now to be feminized. I don't highlight my hair, I've still got a pair, Yea honey I'm still a guy. Oh my eyebrows ain't plucked, there's a gun in my truck. Oh thank God, I'm still a guy."

90. *Business Insider's* Henry Blodget warning that the decline in traditional newspaper readership will only accelerate, "As the generation of consumers who do care about print, meanwhile — the increasingly old people (like me) who grew up on print — continues to age, the pressure on traditional print publications will continue to increase. Time and tide wait for no man. And the media tide is going digital."

91. PayPal co-founder Peter Thiel's effort to prevent graduating high school seniors from enrolling in college by offering $100,000 to those selected and willing to delay college at least two years to focus on entrepreneurship.

92. Maverick Wall Street insider Mike Mayo, who is often critical of the banks he covers as an analyst, becomes a shareholder in the banks he follows for access to investor meetings analysts are normally barred from attending.

93. Rapper Eminem, who has included unflattering lyrics about his estranged mother on past albums, apologizes to his mother in a rap video released on Mother's Day 2014.

94. Oklahoma City journalist Mike McCarville's *The McCarville Report*, a bare knuckled delight of political truth that routinely exposes that which our leaders would rather hide.

95. Former hedge fund manager Andy Kessler's book, *Eat People: And Other Unapologetic Rules for Game-Changing Entrepreneurs*.

96. Steve Borden, otherwise known as the professional wrestler Sting, on the addictions that ultimately led him to accept Jesus Christ as his savior, "I was taking pain killers, I was taking muscle relaxers, and I was drinking alcohol."

97. UFC President Dana White's revelation, "We all get depressed, we all have our moments when things are going great and then you get let down and bad stuff happens. It's about recovering from that, pulling yourself up, dusting yourself off, and get back in the game."

98. Phil Robertson, star of the most watched nonfiction cable television series in history *Duck Dynasty*, stands by comments he made that critics call "anti-gay" and is invited back onto the show after a brief suspension.

99. Peter Bregman in the *Harvard Business Review* on failure, "But when people who have failed are in the depths of despair, they need empathy more than your rationalizations and encouragements about the future… Next time one of your people falls short, listen. Don't interrupt, don't offer advice, don't say that it will be all right. Just reflect back what you hear them say. There will be time to solve the problem later."

100. The scantily clad cardboard cutouts Matthew Epstein sent of himself to Google to get executives to visit a web site he created outlining why the company should hire him. It didn't but others did.

101. Scott Adams, *Dilbert* cartoonist and author, on a topic near and dear to my heart, "These days it seems like any idiot with a laptop computer can churn out a business book and make a few bucks. That's certainly what I'm hoping. It would be a real letdown if the trend changed before this masterpiece goes to print!"

LEAD BY DIRTY EXAMPLE

We want to add to this list, learn from the dirty stories you tell, and feature them for the world to see.

Please share your dirty stories with us at
www.dirtystorytelling.com.

Nick Winkler

THE DIRTY END

Your marketing health hinges upon inspiring belief that spreads.

YOUR DIRTY OBJECTIONS

This book and the ideas in it probably aren't for you.

You'll probably never spend a portion of your marketing budget telling dirty stories. I doubt you'll ever send a news release telling the media how you messed up. And I'm betting most of you will never stand before a crowd and tell it where you fell short.

I hope I'm wrong.

But it's okay if I'm not.

Either way, this book needed to be.

It was conceived 15 years ago when I started out as a television news reporter. It developed over a period marked by an explosion of unbelievable marketing messages. Now, it is born and will be judged either as another of those irrelevant messages or as a story worth doing and spreading.

I'm anxious to see which you choose to believe.

What I believe is that honest, authentic, and valuable stories would make the world a better place if they were told more often. Stories like these would undoubtedly strip much of the cynical skepticism the public has of modern marketing efforts. The telling of dirty stories would allow us to comfortably drop our guards and trust.

The hard part is going first.

Our fear of being first is one that is impossible to get over without doing. But what if the competition laughs at us? What if the trial attorneys hear about this? What if the media run stories about our shortcomings?

It's just safer not to go first.

Dirty Storytelling

So we don't.

The dirty story I'll tell you is that anyone could've written this book. While unique, this book isn't special in the sense that it doesn't provide a secret groundbreaking marketing shortcut guaranteed to work for everyone overnight.

It simply examines some of the lessons we learned as children through the lens of a marketer.

Many of us learned as children we were much better off volunteering to our parents we had gotten into trouble rather than waiting for the babysitter, principal, or police officer to tell on us. To our surprise we learned our parents admired our integrity which earned us goodwill not available to those who don't acknowledge their transgressions. Telling on ourselves often resulted in lighter punishments than would have been meted out otherwise.

School taught us this isn't always the case though. College reinforced our choice to hide our blemishes. And the world of work taught us admitting fault would result in not being promoted.

So we bury the lessons of our childhood.

In their place we stick expensive bandages that cover but do not heal.

We choose marketers to tell us how we should talk to prospects. We choose public relations firms to tell us what to say to the media. We choose reputation managers to tell us how to hide criticism.

What if we chose the truth instead?

The one we live.

Besides saving money we might also rediscover the lessons of our childhood. The same types of admissions that made our parents proud of us might also cause customers to feel similarly. The benefit of the doubt our courage earned us as children may earn us similar slack with those we wish to influence commercially.

Understand that choosing the truth doesn't mean we don't tell it in a way that is favorable to our reputation. However, positioning our truths in ways that benefit others will ultimately benefit us as well.

But it's career suicide, we're told, to admit we've been wrong. We've been conditioned not to talk about our problems. Changing course, at least publicly, is an admission we've been wasting time and money. So just like professional fighters, we feign strength when we are weak.

That's smart if you're in a fistfight.

But what if displaying your fallibility for the benefit of others is actually a sign of strength?

We're all dirty storytellers, we just don't all tell dirty stories.

Not convinced?

Rapists, child molesters, and Ponzi scheme operators routinely provide relatively honest accounts of their behavior after they've been exposed. Initially, I was shocked as a television news reporter when I confronted people accused of horrific behavior and they readily admitted, confessed, or apologized for their actions on camera.

Dirty Storytelling

While not everyone confessed, the majority still told their stories. The one they believed. They justified their questionable behavior, explained why they had to do what they did, or otherwise attempted to convince the world their intentions were good even if their actions were not.

Why?

No one thinks they're bad.

Even people who knowingly do bad things believe they have good reasons for doing them. If only the world understood, they tell themselves, it would understand why I did what I did.

I've learned if you give people a good reason to tell their story they often will, even if it's not in their interest to do so. This is often how law enforcement officers get criminals to confess. It's how social workers get child abuse victims to finally open up and talk. And it's why people living in the U.S. illegally feel comfortable holding public demonstrations in support of amnesty.

Nearly everyone who is given a good reason to do so will tell their story honestly, or as they see it.

Except, it seems, organizations that should do so.

Remember, criminals, scammers, and manipulators tell their stories even when they should not. But you have a good reason to tell your story. And doing so is also in your interest.

So what's stopping you other than fear?

Objection: We're already telling dirty stories. We apologize when we make a mistake, respond to criticism on social media, and take pride in our honest customer service.

Response: Well done but you're simply reacting as the majority does. Dirty stories are different in that they are proactive. Dirty storytellers tell on themselves rather than waiting and seemingly being forced to do so. The power inherent in dirty stories is that they create a first mover advantage generally reserved for prosecutors. Dirty stories establish an organization as the primary narrator of the story rather than a supporting role. Dirty stories make headlines, rules, and agendas rather than responding to them.

Objection: I'm not a storyteller nor do I need to be, so dirty stories are something I just don't need.

Response: If you're in business you've signed up to be a storyteller whether you like it or not. We are wired to tell stories. Stories allow us to create meaning, share it, and navigate a complex world. If you opt out of storytelling you allow others to create the story by which you'll be judged regardless of whether it is accurate. This is a risk no one who has shed blood, sweat, and tears turning their dream into a reality needs to take. While the types of stories you'll tell depend on your industry, to whom you sell, and how you make those transactions, your livelihood still depends, in part, on the story you tell. So why would you tell stories like everyone else? If you're going to tell stories you might as well tell the best. The dirtiest. You routinely upgrade your equipment, software, and skill set just to keep up with the competition. Upgrade your storytelling and get ahead.

Objection: Nick, you're the only one talking about dirty stories. Why should I believe you or that this will work?
Response: The very fact that dirty stories are rare is exactly why you should start telling them. We are wired to notice the atypical and dirty stories are just that. You want to be noticed, right? Dirty storytelling is marketing's dirty little secret. Dirty stories are being told but not en masse. One of the hardest parts of this book to write was the 101 examples of dirty stories. They're extremely difficult to find. As a television news reporter, I received at least a quarter million news releases during my career. Less than one percent was dirty. It's why I never acted on the majority and deleted the rest. The question you have to answer is what do you want to be; the haystack or the needle?

Objection: We mess up a lot, Nick. What are we supposed to do, hold a news conference every time we fail, make a mistake, or fall short?
Response: Not at all. While I certainly advocate airing your dirty laundry for the benefit of those you wish to influence, you don't need to air it all. Dirty storytelling is a technique to be used strategically. Not every story you tell must be dirty. However, the believability, trust,

and goodwill you earn by telling dirty stories will bleed over into your other marketing efforts. The credibility you earn by telling dirty stories is transferable to a degree. In other words, you'll get credit for being dirty even when you're not.

The next time you catch your toes curling in hopes that the mishap you just experienced remains private, think a bit deeper about the blunder.

More importantly, examine your reaction to the mishap.

I'm betting your reaction to the gaffe, unless you're grossly negligent or have acted with malice, is one of which you are proud.

It would be a shame to continue to hide these reactions. They are valuable to you and those you wish to influence. Consider displaying these reactions for the benefit of others.

It won't be appropriate every time.

But you'll be surprised at how much more authentic and effective your marketing will become when you allow a little dirt to color it. This is the kind of truth people relentlessly pursue. It's the kind that is rewarded with attention, belief, and business.

When you scrub it from your story you cheat us all.

Even worse, you hurt yourself.

Remember, science teaches that cleansing, scrubbing, and sanitizing too much can actually reduce the potency of that which heals, make us sick, and even kill us.

Dirty Storytelling

The same is true of the stories we tell.

A bit of dirt is actually good for our stories. It prevents them from becoming belief-resistant and makes our marketing lives healthier. To remain healthy, you must inspire belief that spreads.

To do so will require making difficult choices; maintain the status quo or experiment with something that causes you fear and discomfort?

Lead with cowardice or courage?

Position yourself as perfectly ignorable or imperfectly necessary?

Tell dirty stories.

Nick Winkler

NICK WINKLER

Nick Winkler is founder of *The Winkler Group*, which helps individuals and organizations ignite growth with story. He is the author of three books, a blog, and creator of an online network of strategic communications resources.

In a previous life, Nick was an investigative and general assignment television news reporter whose work has been featured on ABC, CNN, Fox News, and network affiliates nationwide.

Visit **www.thewinklergroup.net** for additional detail, ideas, and free storytelling resources.

DIRTY
STORYTELLING
Market with Mud

Nick Winkler

Visit **THE DIRTY STORYTELLING**
website for additional ideas, handbooks,
and resources.

www.dirtystorytelling.com

THE WINKLER GROUP
STRATEGIC COMMUNICATIONS

Ignite growth with story.

www.thewinklergroup.net